Urban and Regional Economics

ECONOMICS INFORMATION GUIDE SERIES

Series Editor: Robert W. Haseltine, Associate Professor of Economics, State University College of Arts and Science at Geneseo, New York

Also in this series:

AMERICAN ECONOMIC HISTORY—*Edited by William K. Hutchinson**

EAST ASIAN ECONOMIES—*Edited by Molly K.S.C. Lee*

ECONOMIC EDUCATION—*Edited by Catherine A. Hughes*

ECONOMIC HISTORY OF CANADA—*Edited by Trevor J.O. Dick*

ECONOMICS OF MINORITIES—*Edited by Kenneth L. Gagala*

HEALTH AND MEDICAL ECONOMICS—*Edited by Ted J. Ackroyd*

HISTORY OF ECONOMIC ANALYSIS—*Edited by William K. Hutchinson*

LABOR ECONOMICS—*Edited by Ross E. Azevedo*

MATHEMATICAL ECONOMICS AND OPERATIONS RESEARCH—*Edited by Joseph Zaremba*

MONEY, BANKING, AND MACROECONOMICS—*Edited by James Rock*

REGIONAL STATISTICS—*Edited by M. Balachandran*

RUSSIAN ECONOMIC HISTORY—*Edited by Daniel R. Kazmer and Vera Kazmer*

SOVIET-TYPE ECONOMIC SYSTEMS—*Edited by Z. Edward O'Relley*

STATISTICS AND ECONOMETRICS—*Edited by Joseph Zaremba**

TRANSPORTATION ECONOMICS—*Edited by James P. Rakowski*

*in preparation

The above series is part of the
GALE INFORMATION GUIDE LIBRARY

The Library consists of a number of separate series of guides covering major areas in the social sciences, humanities, and current affairs.

General Editor: Paul Wasserman, Professor and former Dean, School of Library and Information Services, University of Maryland

Managing Editor: Denise Allard Adzigian, Gale Research Company

Urban and Regional Economics

A GUIDE TO INFORMATION SOURCES

Volume 14 in the Economics Information Guide Series

Jean A. Shackelford

Assistant Professor
Bucknell University
Lewisburg, Pennsylvania

Gale Research Company
Book Tower, Detroit, Michigan 48226

Library of Congress Cataloging in Publication Data

Shackelford, Jean A
    Urban and regional economics.

    (Economics information guide series ; v. 14)
(Gale information guide library)
    Includes bibliographies and indexes.
    1. Regional economics—Bibliography. 2. Urban
economics—Bibliography. I. Title.
Z7164.R33S48   [HT321]   016.3309173'2   74-11556
ISBN 0-8103-1303-0

VITA

Jean A. Shackelford is an assistant professor in economics at Bucknell University, where she specializes in economic theory, monetary economics, and the history of economic thought. Dr. Shackelford received her B.A. in economics from Kansas State University and her M.A. and Ph.D. from the University of Kentucky. She is also interested in international economics and women in the economy and has delivered many papers on these topics for various economics associations throughout the country.

Dr. Shackelford is a coauthor of ECONOMICS: A TOOL FOR UNDERSTANDING SOCIETY (Reading, Mass.: Addison Wesley Publishing Co., 1979) and is currently working under a grant from the Department of Health, Education and Welfare on "Women in Professional and Managerial Work Roles: A Program of Education and Experience for College Students."

CONTENTS

ACKNOWLEDGMENTS

A number of people were extremely helpful and supportive as I have churned through this work. Library staffs across the country have been generous with suggestions and with the use of their facilities. The staff at the Library of Congress, I'm sure unknowingly, made my work easier with the accessibility of the collection. The Bucknell library staff has been extremely generous. I would particularly like to thank reference librarians Nancy Books and Nancy Weyant who have the ability to track down just about anything, no matter how hazy the reference, and George Jenks, the university librarian, whose signature opened stacks and encouragement provided momentum at difficult times. Most of all, of course, I must thank my husband, Ron Brinkman, for his patience, tolerance, and help with Brian, who, at two going on three, knows neither of these.

PREFACE

This volume has been designed to aid scholars in both research and teaching activities in the areas of urban and regional economics. No doubt it will be useful to others as well who are interested in various aspects of urban and regional economics: students, planners, government officials, and interested lay people. Some 600 books are listed and are divided by these two broad categories. No attempt was made to include journal articles, since, in the case of several journals, this would involve listing every article that has ever been published in them. Instead, the reader will find a list of journals in urban and regional economics as well as journals of a more general nature which often publish titles of interest in the appendix. In addition, there is a listing of publishers with special series devoted to work in these areas.

Some parts of this work are more complete than others. Some parts contain titles relevant to both areas or to more than one subheading. In these two fields it is often difficult to classify work according to a single category. In cases where such a determination was difficult, the topic which seemed to dominate was used to classify. The section on urban history is far from thorough, and the devotion to economics in these listings is in most cases marginal. The section is included for those interested in, and needing relevant background material for, studies in regional and urban growth.

While urban and regional economics are directly related to areas of housing, transportation, urban renewal, pollution, poverty, and other specific area studies, these have not been included unless the emphasis of the work was specifically an urban or regional economics title or if that proved to be the major thrust of the work. Hence, URBANIZATION, WATER POLLUTION, and PUBLIC POLICY is included and THE POLITICS OF NEGLECT: URBAN AID FROM MODEL CITIES TO REVENUE SHARING is not. There is also an overlap in coverage of these areas by various disciplines in the social sciences. Some sociology and political science books on the city which have an economic bias are included, as are many books in the field of urban geography, where discussion of location theory and spatial analysis totally overlap those found in regional economics.

Preface

Although the volume itself is reasonably complete, there are of course omissions, and for that I apologize. Note cards keep popping out of strange places, and old and new references and citations come to my attention even as I write this preface. My first question in starting this endeavor was: "Where do I begin?" It has now become: "Where do I end?"

There are a few listings for which no annotations appear. These have somehow escaped a very capable and diligent interlibrary loan staff as well as the shelves of the Library of Congress. They are listed with the hope that they will be acquired by those who are particularly interested.

As in other volumes in this series, annotations give the views of the author as to the purpose, goal, and objectives of the work, as stated in the preface, introduction, or cover notes, or as conveyed in the table of contents. No attempt has been made to judge the success or failure of the authors in their stated mission.

LIST OF ABBREVIATIONS

ARA	Area Redevelopment Administration
ARC	Appalachian Regional Commission
CED	Committee for Economic Development
EDA	Economic Development Administration
EEC	European Economic Community
I-O	Input-Output
L.P.	Linear Programing
NBER	National Bureau of Economic Research
NTIT	New Towns Intown
NUE	New Urban Economics
OECD	Organization for Economic Cooperation and Development
QJE	Quarterly Journal of Economics
RFF	Resources for the Future
SSRC	Social Science Research Council

Part I

URBAN ECONOMICS

Chapter 1
HISTORICAL ASPECTS OF URBANIZATION

Abrams, Charles. THE CITY IS THE FRONTIER. New York: Harper and Row, 1965. xii, 394 p.

> A review of urban renewal written for the Ford Foundation, this work views the problems of slums and how past urban renewal policies have dealt with them. The final section of the book is devoted to the needs of slum areas and the political accommodation of these needs in a macro perspective.

Allen, James B. THE COMPANY TOWN IN THE AMERICAN WEST. Norman: University of Oklahoma Press, 1966. xviii, 222 p.

> An examination of the history and development of the single base company town in the frontier. Factors which receive examination are management, economics, politics, and paternalism. Location and prevailing attitudes are examined in this historical context as are advances in communications and transportation.

Anderson, Nels. THE INDUSTRIAL URBAN COMMUNITY: HISTORICAL AND COMPARATIVE PERSPECTIVES. New York: Appleton-Century-Crofts, 1971. xii, 438 p. Index, pp. 423-38.

> While this book is a historical approach to urban sociology, there might be several chapters of interest to those needing introductory treatment of urban communities and their function, evolution, ecology, and mobility. In addition to discussions on urban life and people, planning, technical change, and the behavior of urban agglomerations are examined.

Barth, Gunther. INSTANT CITIES: URBANIZATION AND THE RISE OF SAN FRANCISCO AND DENVER. New York: Oxford University Press, 1975. xviii, 310 p. Sources, pp. 233-42. Notes, pp. 243-302. Index, pp. 303-10.

> The rapid growth of these two cities in the nineteenth century is contrasted with three other types of settlements. The early U.S. urban experience is treated with discussions of the "Minimum of

3

Order," "Reluctant Cities," "Culture for the Moment," and "Technology Stimulates Transition."

Beckinsale, R.P., and Houston, J.M., eds. URBANIZATION AND ITS PROBLEMS. Oxford: Basil Blackwell, 1968. xvii, 443 p.

This is a comprehensive view of urbanization from 1420 onward. The origin and development of town life is discussed on an international scale, from Europe to China, the USSR and South Africa.

Bender, Thomas. TOWARD AN URBAN VISION: IDEAS AND INSTITUTIONS IN 19TH-CENTURY AMERICA. Lexington: University of Kentucky Press, 1975. 292 p. Index.

This historical volume seeks to explain the changing or new ideologies which developed to justify the meaning of urban life which the older belief systems no longer provided.

Billan, Ruben C. THE EVOLVING CITY. New York: Pitman Publishing Corp., 1971. 420 p. Index, pp. 409-20. Illus.

Three main parts are extensively developed to frame this discussion of the evolution of urban areas. The history of cities is examined from the first cities to twentieth-century cities. Next Billan introduces the role and "Evolution of Municipal Government Functions." The discussion then turns to the "City in the National Economy" where national urban networks and regional balance are examined.

Callow, Alexander B., Jr., ed. AMERICAN URBAN HISTORY: AN INTERPRETATIVE READER WITH COMMENTARIES. New York: Oxford University Press, 1969. xii, 674 p. No Index.

The purpose of this anthology was to bring together a group of diverse essays that "illuminate the important themes and problems in urban history." The approach is an interdisciplinary one, and the essays are arranged chronologically and topically. Areas which are covered include "The City in History," "The City in Colonial America," "The City in the Era of: Manifest Destiny, Industry, and Transition," and "The City in Modern Times."

Chudacoff, Howard P. THE EVOLUTION OF AMERICAN URBAN SOCIETY. Englewood Cliffs, N.J.: Prentice-Hall, 1975. viii, 280 p. Index, pp. 270-80.

The author's aim is to trace a path of American urban history which focuses on areas of recent interest in the field. The emphasis is on the growth and evolution of cities and urban networks and their evolution. The U.S. city is examined from the colonial period through 1975.

4

Fisher, Robert Moore, ed. THE METROPOLIS IN MODERN LIFE. Garden City, N.Y.: Doubleday, 1955. 401 p. Index, pp. 391–401.

There are 22 essays which focus on the growth of the city over the past 200 years.

Glaab, Charles Nelson. THE AMERICAN CITY: A DOCUMENTARY HISTORY. Homewood, Ill.: Dorsey Press, 1963. xiv, 478 p. Suggested Readings, pp. 475–78. No index.

Case studies from U.S. urban development are included in this historical analysis of the growth of cities.

Green, Constance McLaughlin. AMERICAN CITIES IN THE GROWTH OF THE NATION. New York: Harper and Row, 1957. xii, 258 p.

This is a historical representation of the maturing nation from east to west and the establishment of towns and urban areas.

Handlin, Oscar, and Burchard, John, eds. THE HISTORIAN AND THE CITY. Cambridge: M.I.T. Press and Harvard University Press, 1963. xii, 299 p. Index, pp. 291–99.

This is a compilation of papers resulting from a conference in 1961 sponsored by the Joint Center for Urban Studies at M.I.T. and Harvard to consider the city in history. Contributors include A. Gerschenkron, K. Boulding, and E. Lamphard.

Healy, Patrick III. THE NATION'S CITIES. New York: Harper and Row, 1974. xiii, 288 p. Notes, pp. 267–75. Index, pp. 276–88.

This is a chronicle of the changes encountered in cities within the last 50 years. The book traces the city in the United States to its colonial origins but devotes most of its attention to the period since the 1920s. The ups and downs of each decade are recounted.

Holli, Melvin G., ed. DETROIT. Documentary History of American Cities Series. New York: New Viewpoints, 1976. 288 p. Paper.

This group of essays deals with the entire history of Detroit's rise from a French outpost to a large industrial city.

Jackson, Kenneth T., and Schultz, Stanley K., eds. CITIES IN AMERICAN HISTORY. New York: Alfred A. Knopf, 1972. xi, 508 p. Bibliography, pp. 492–506. No index.

This collection of readings was designed for supplemental use in courses in urban history or urban studies. It is interdisciplinary in nature and is designed to acquaint students with a large sample of recent interpretive studies. There are 27 essays which are grouped into seven broad parts. These include: "The City in American History," "Cities in the New World 1607-1800," "Cities in an Expanding Nation," "Immigration, Migration, and Mobility 1865-1920," "The Recurrent Urban Crisis," "Bosses, Machines and Urban Reform," and "The Dilemmas of Metropolitan America."

Jroen, Selwyn K., and Holt, Glen E., eds. ST. LOUIS. Documentary History of American Cities Series. New York: New Viewpoints, 1977. 288 p.

Economic development and demographic change are the focus of these essays on St. Louis. The problems of growth, innovations in planning, and the role of the city in the region and the nation are highlighted.

Klein, Maury, and Kantor, Harvey A. PRISONERS OF PROGRESS: AMERICAN INDUSTRIAL CITIES, 1850-1920. xvii, 459 p. Index, pp. 443-59.

This book deals with the dominant forces at work in the period of industrial-urban growth between 1850 and 1920.

Larsen, Lawrence H. THE URBAN WEST AT THE END OF THE FRONTIER. Lawrence: Regents Press of Kansas, 1978. xiv, 173 p.

This is a portrayal of western urban life complete with planners, crowding lots into tracts, crowded conditions, and late nineteenth-century technology. Over 20 specific cities are examined regarding their function and form. It is a multidisciplinary discussion.

Lindstrom, Diane. ECONOMIC DEVELOPMENT IN THE PHILADELPHIA REGION, 1810-1850. New York: Columbia University Press, 1978. xi, 255 p. Notes, pp. 203-33. Selected bibliography, pp. 233-44. Index, pp. 245-55.

The period Lindstrom views is one in which there were several "distinct regional economies" in the U.S. She deals with this "statistical dark age" examining the rise and development of the Philadelphia region in its response to economic change. Chapters discuss: "American Economic Development, 1815-1940," "From Commerce to Manufacturing: Economic Transformation Within Philadelphia County," "In Pursuit of Markets and Trade: Philadelphia's Extraregional Commerce," "Interregional Trade and Transport Innovation: Philadelphia and its Hinterland," "Integration into a Regional Economy: Economic Development within the Hinterland," and "Reaping the Benefits of Specialization."

Lubove, Roy, ed. PITTSBURGH. Documentary History of American Cities Series. New York: New Viewpoints, 1976. 288 p. Paper.

The prologue traces the development of Pittsburgh from 1820-1866. The book then deals with three additional periods: "The Age of Iron and Steel, 1860-1914," "Maturity and Obsolescence, 1914-

45," and "Renaissance." Each part deals with the city's economic development, class, and cultural aspects of growth.

McKelvey, Blake. THE EMERGENCE OF METROPOLITAN AMERICA. New Brunswick, N.J.: Rutgers University Press, 1968. xi, 311 p. Notes, pp. 255-96. Bibliographical note, pp. 297-300. Index, pp. 301-11.

A "continuation" of THE URBANIZATION OF AMERICA, McKelvey begins in 1915 to explore the "new stage" of American urbanization. The approach toward urban growth is historical and "seeks to place the changing networks and national relationships in time and place perspective." Chapters include: "The Emerging Metropolitan Dilemmas: 1915-20," "An Outburst of Metropolitan Initiative: 1920-29," "The Discovery of Metropolitan Inadequacy: 1930-39," "The Metropolis in War and Peace: 1940-49," "The Metropolis and the Establishment: 1950-59," and "Federal-Metropolitan Convergence in the 60's."

_____. THE URBANIZATION OF AMERICA (1860-1915). New Brunswick, N.J.: Rutgers University Press, 1963. xii, 370 p. Notes, pp. 287-331. Bibliography, pp. 333-58. Index, pp. 359-70.

McKelvey begins by discussing the "second, more complicated stage of urbanization" which the United States had reached by 1860, including technical advances, population growth, and resource and geographical expansion. He builds and continues on this stage through 1915.

Martin, Robert L. THE CITY MOVES WEST: ECONOMIC AND INDUSTRIAL GROWTH IN CENTRAL WEST TEXAS. Austin: University of Texas Press, 1969. vi, 190 p.

This is an examination of the importance of urban areas and urban development in West Texas. The economic factors responsible for this growth are presented along with a model and a historical survey of the area.

Mumford, Lewis. THE CITY IN HISTORY. New York: Harcourt, Brace and World, 1961. xi, 657 p. Bibliography, pp. 579-636. Index, pp. 637-57.

This is a historical epic of the rise of the city from ancient and medieval periods of our own suburban condition. Mumford deals with the forms and functions of cities and the purposes that have emerged from them.

_____. THE URBAN PROSPECT. New York: Harcourt, Brace and World, 1956. xx, 255 p.

This collection of Mumford's essays were written between 1950 and 1956 and examines the prospect for urban development.

Queen, Stuart Alfred, and Thomas, Lewis Francis. THE CITY: A STUDY OF URBANISM IN THE UNITED STATES. New York: McGraw-Hill, 1939. xv, 515 p. Index, pp. 500-515.

> This is a thorough sociological and geographical look at the methods and patterns of urban-rural movements. Economic factors relating to cycles, base, and location theory are examined along with cultural and institutional factors within urban and rural areas.

Roebuck, Janet. THE SHAPING OF URBAN SOCIETY: A HISTORY OF CITY FORMS AND FUNCTIONS. New York: Charles Scribner's Sons, 1974. x, 256 p. Bibliography, pp. 237-47. Index, pp. 247-56. Illus.

> This volume offers a general historical background of the city in history from the medieval city to the modern city. It is written partly for "other specialists" with a need for a general historical background of the city.

Schnore, Leo F., ed. THE NEW URBAN HISTORY. Princeton, N.J.: Princeton University Press, 1975. ix, 284 p. Index, pp. 277-84.

> This third volume of a Mathematical Social Science Board Study in History deals with the process of urbanization in the United States in primarily the nineteenth and early twentieth century. Quantitative techniques are simple and straight forward. Topic areas of the nine essays include: the growth and functions of cities, accommodations to the urban environment, and economic analyses of urban-historical phenomena.

Strauss, Anselm L. IMAGES OF THE AMERICAN CITY. New York: Free Press of Glencoe, 1961. xiv, 306 p. Notes, pp. 259-98. Index, pp. 299-306.

> Economic history gives this monograph on the city its focus. From the early "agrarian vision" to the rise of cities, Strauss views urban history in an economic and sociological context.

Wakstein, Allen M., ed. THE URBANIZATION OF AMERICA: A HISTORICAL ANTHOLOGY. Boston: Houghton-Mifflin, 1970. ix, 501 p. Bibliography, pp. 491-501. No index.

> A wide variety of subjects related to urbanization are included in this anthology, from the physical growth of cities to political, economic, and social change factors. The eight major sections are on: "The Study of Urbanization" (four essays), "The Establishment and Growth of Urban Centers" (four essays), "The Growth and Development of Urban Services" (four essays), "Urbanization and Industrialization" (four essays), "The Impact of Urbanization" (five essays), "The Rising Concern for Urban Life" (four essays), "Metropolitanization" (five essays), and "Contemporary Urban Problems" (seven essays).

Weber, Adna Ferrin. GROWTH OF CITIES IN THE NINETEENTH CENTURY: A STUDY IN STATISTICS. New York: Macmillan Co. for Columbia University, 1899. xvi, 495 p. Bibliographic Notes, pp. 476–78. Index of Authors, pp. 479–82. Index of Subjects, pp. 483–95.

This is an impressive statistical examination of the growth of the world's urban areas, given data limitations in 1899. Urban growth and structure in the nineteenth century is given extensive treatment, including examinations of migration, economic conditions, and the economic effects of agglomeration.

Chapter 2

PERSPECTIVES ON URBAN AREAS: VIEWS AND ISSUES

Banfield, Edward C. THE UNHEAVENLY CITY: THE NATURE AND FUTURE OF OUR URBAN CRISES. 2d ed. Boston: Little, Brown and Co., 1970. xiii, 321 p.

> Banfield uses the social sciences perspective in the quest for betterment of the city. He redefines the nature of the problem and, thus, finds new solutions for these "new" traditional problems. This book has been surrounded by a great deal of controversy since its initial publication.

_____. THE UNHEAVENLY CITY REVISITED. Boston: Little, Brown and Co., 1974. xii, 358 p.

> This is another look at THE UNHEAVENLY CITY which attempts to clarify and add new data and developments to Banfield's earlier work.

Berry, Brian J.L. THE HUMAN CONSEQUENCES OF URBANIZATION. London: Macmillan Press, 1973. xv, 205 p. Bibliography. Index.

> The historic patterns of urbanization from the Industrial Revolution through the twentieth century are examined in this book. Urban patterns in the Third World, European planning, and patterns of the future are given particular emphasis. Divergent paths are explored as well, and emphasis is on the varying political, economic, and social structures.

Blair, Thomas G. THE INTERNATIONAL URBAN CRISIS. New York: Hill and Wang, 1974. 176 p.

> The urban explosion is examined on the international level as to what occurred and what went wrong. Traditional problems are discussed, including slums, decay, sprawl, pollution, new towns, and planning.

Clay, Grady. CLOSE-UP: HOW TO READ THE AMERICAN CITY. New York: Praeger, 1973. 192 p. Notes, pp. 182-88. Index, pp. 189-92. Illus.

> Grady has come up with a new vocabulary to examine the city in its social and economic perspectives and to "grasp the visual evidence of the processes at work that convert the past to the future." This new language is apparent in the book's chapters on: "Wordgame," "Fixes," "Epitome Districts," "Fronts," "Beats," "Sinks," "Turf," and "Vantages."

Committee for Economic Development. RESHAPING GOVERNMENT IN THE METROPOLITAN AREA. New York: 1970. 88 p. No index.

> This essay discusses government expenditure and its impact on citizens of urban areas. The argument presented here is that the existing metropolitan government organization does not recognize the problems of both the central city and the suburban areas. It also discusses the argument that there is a need for both community and metropolitan government.

_____. GUIDING METROPOLITAN GROWTH. New York: 1960. 50 p. No index.

> This is a policy statement of the CED on urban America which recommends: careful studies of the economic base of communities, the recasting of urban renewal programs in terms of conserving middle-aged and older residential neighborhoods, and reorganizing government in metropolitan areas to be more efficient and effective.

Fitch, Lyle Craig. THE POLITICAL ECONOMY OF URBAN SYSTEMS. Los Angeles: Institute of Government and Public Affairs, University of California, 1971. 46 p. Bibliographical references.

> This is Fitch's "regents lecture" presented at UCLA in February 1971. It is primarily a general discussion of urban problems.

Funigiello, Philip J. THE CHALLENGE TO URBAN LIBERALISM: FEDERAL-CITY RELATIONS DURING WORLD WAR II. Knoxville: University of Tennessee Press, 1978. 276 p. Index.

> The author asserts that the federal government's failure to develop a more comprehensive urban policy during, and in the period immediately after, World War II has resulted in the extreme seriousness of the urban crisis today.

Glazer, Nathan, ed. CITIES IN TROUBLE. Chicago: Quadrangle Books, 1970. 276 p. Suggested Readings, pp. 269-71. Index, pp. 271-76.

> Glazer, H. Gans, J. Willson, I. Kustol, D. Moynehan, C. Jencks, P. Goodman, and N. Mailer are contributors to this volume. The

five topic categories for the essays are: "Nature of the Crises,"
"How Bad is It," "The Negro and the Immigrant," "Solutions,"
"New York in 1969."

Griffin, C.W. TAMING THE LAST FRONTIER: A PRESCRIPTION FOR THE
URBAN CRISIS. New York: Pitman Publishing Corp., 1974. xii, 260 p.

This work argues for institutional changes to deal with our urban
environmental disasters. Air pollution, traffic, population growth,
and sprawl are viewed from an engineering problem solving perspective.

Hall, Peter. THE WORLD CITIES. New York: McGraw-Hill, 1966. 256 p.
Bibliography, pp. 246-54. Index, pp. 255-56. Illus.

Hall examines the growth of seven large metropolitan complexes
throughout the world, looking at the causes behind the growth,
the problems created by it, and the attempts which have been
made to solve these problems. The focus is on the "general forces"
which are at work in most urban areas. These include population
increases, a shift in the economic base from industry to services,
and concentration. The cities examined in depth are London; Paris;
Randstad, Holland; Moscow; New York City; and Tokyo.

Hallenbeck, Wilbur C. AMERICAN URBAN COMMUNITIES. New York:
Harper and Row, 1951. xi, 617 p. Name index, pp. 601-03. Subject index,
pp. 604-17.

Herbert, Lewis [Bookchin, Murray]. THE LIMITS OF THE CITY. New York:
Harper and Row, 1974. xi, 147 p. Index, pp. 140-47.

This essay takes a historical perspective in the examination of the
development of the city, the traditions of urbanism, and a perspective on what the city was once like. It is highly critical of
the standards of city life today and establishes these low standards
as the roots of the urban crisis.

Hoyt, Homer. WHERE THE RICH AND POOR LIVE. Washington, D.C.: Urban
Land Institute, 1966. 64 p. No index.

This study utilized 1960 Census data to examine the location of
high-, middle-, and low-income families. There is a detailed
analysis of high-income areas in selected standard metropolitan
areas as well as the location of low-income families in American
cities.

Jacobs, Jane. THE DEATH AND LIFE OF GREAT AMERICAN CITIES. New
York: Vintage Books, 1961. 458 p. Index, pp. 449-58.

This book represents one of Jacob's earliest attacks on current city planning, rebuilding and on the principles and aims that have shaped the modern city. There are 22 chapters and four principle parts to her argument. The first centers on "The Particular Nature of Cities," the second "The Conditions for City Diversity," the third, "Forces of Decline and Regeneration," and, in conclusion, she offers her own solutions in "Different Tactics."

_____. THE ECONOMY OF CITIES. New York: Random House, 1969. 268 p. Index, pp. 263–68.

This book offers Jacob's analysis of why some cities grow and some decline. Her argument is that it's the innumerable, unpredictable offshoots that "break away from and often replace established corporations" which proliferate and add to the sum of all economic activity. The eight chapters discuss: "Cities First, Rural Development Later," "How New Work Begins," "The Valuable Inefficient and Impracticalities of Cities," "How Cities Start Growing," "Explosive City Growth," "How Large Cities Generate Exports," "Capital for City Economic Development," and "Some Patterns of Future Development." Several appendixes follow.

Liston, Robert A. DOWNTOWN OUR CHALLENGING URBAN PROBLEMS. New York: Delacorte Press, 1965. 173 p.

This is a newspaper reporter's insights into urban problems, their nature, and potential solutions.

Long, Norton E. THE UNWALLED CITY: RECONSTITUTING THE URBAN COMMUNITY. New York: Basic Books, 1972. 208 p.

In this book, Long views employment as the key to the health of the city and argues that a viable local economy must be used to assure this. He argues that past growth and imported expenditures are not the solutions for urban revitalization.

McQuade, Walter. CITIES FIT TO LIVE IN AND HOW WE CAN MAKE THEM HAPPEN. New York: Macmillan Co., 1971. viii, 152 p.

An urban planner's look at urban problems of crime, violence, the environment, and zoning and the issues of poverty and urban disorders.

Morris, Richard S. BUM RAP ON AMERICAN CITIES: THE REAL CAUSES OF URBAN DECAY. Englewood Cliffs, N.J.: Prentice-Hall, 1978. vi, 198 p. Notes, 189–94. Index, pp. 195–98.

The liberals, argues Morris, are taking the "bum rap" in shouldering the blame for the fiscal and economic decay of the American city." He then contrasts the "real issues" with the "myths" and offers solutions to the urban ills. The villains? Planned federal policy and expenditure in the rural West and South.

Moynihan, Daniel P., ed. TOWARD A NATIONAL URBAN POLICY. New York: Basic Books, 1970. xiv, 362 p. Index, pp. 348.

Topics under examination are the traditional ones: population, housing, transportation, land use, health, pollution, poverty, renewal, new towns and the like. Essays by P. Hauser, J. Kain, J. Meyer and other social scientists were written out of concern for urban areas.

Natural Resources Committee. OUR CITIES: ROLE IN THE NATIONAL ECONOMY. Washington, D.C.: Government Printing Office, 1937. xiv, 87 p.

This report is from the first major study of cities in the United States. The problems created by the population shift from rural to urban areas are examined, including the inequalities in income distribution, wealth, transportation, public health, and growth. This examination led to policy recommendations.

Reissman, Leonard. THE URBAN PROCESS: CITIES IN INDUSTRIAL SOCIETIES. New York: Free Press of Glencoe, 1964. xiv, 255 p. Notes, pp. 239-48. Index, pp. 249-55.

Reissman's purpose in this undertaking was to "analyze critically the information about urban society for a theory of urban society." It sets up a "framework for research and construction of a theory of urbanization." Chapters include the examination of "Urban Achievement," "A Typology of Urban Studies," "The Visionary: Planner for Urban Utopia," "The Empiricists: Classifiers of Cities," "The Ecologists: Analysts of Urban Patterns," "The Theoreticians: Developers of the Urban Concept," "The Scope of an Urban Society," and "The City in an Industrial Society."

Toynbee, Arnold. CITIES ON THE MOVE. New York: Oxford University Press, 1970. ix, 257 p.

This work is an examination of "the urban explosion occurring throughout the world and the growth of the 'world city' which spreads its tenacles around the globe."

Weaver, Robert C. THE URBAN COMPLEX, HUMAN VALUES IN URBAN LIFE. Garden City, N.Y.: Doubleday and Co., 1964. xii, 297 p.

From a history of the urban frontier to examples of then current urban economic policy, this book examines the goals and values of urban renewal, fiscal policy and the cities, FHA, FNMA and housing, manpower programs, new towns, and urban planning.

Chapter 3

URBAN GROWTH AND DEVELOPMENT

Andrews, Richard B. URBAN GROWTH AND DEVELOPMENT: A PROBLEM APPROACH. New York: Simmons-Bordman Publishing Corp., 1962. x, 420 p. Index.

Urban growth and development is approached from a variety of disciplines. The economy of cities is reviewed, and an examination of urban transportation, housing, race, poverty, education, and crime is made.

_____. URBAN LAND ECONOMICS AND PUBLIC POLICY. New York: Free Press, 1971. x, 159 p.

This multidisciplinary approach to the problem of land use examines prevailing patterns and visions in the context of legal systems and the attempt to regulate land use. Economic and social factors are considered.

Applebaum, Richard P.; Bigelow, Jenifer; Kramer, Henry P.; Molotch, Harvey L.; and Riles, Paul M. THE EFFECTS OF URBAN GROWTH: A POPULATION IMPACT ANALYSIS. New York: Praeger, 1976. xx, 331 p. Bibliography, pp. 319-30.

This is an analysis designed to determine the optimum level of population for a city. It is comprehensive, and the authors hope it might serve as a model for others wishing to study the question of growth. The book presents an analysis of the effects of growth on the city with respect to its economic well-being. The economic effects of both the private and public sectors are examined, as are the ways in which the changing economic base of a community alters the costs and benefits to the community.

Archer, R.W. URBAN DEVELOPMENT SYSTEMS: NOTES FOR A COURSE OF LECTURES ON THE ECONOMICS OF URBAN DEVELOPMENT. Canberra: Canberra College of Advanced Education, 1972. 28 p. Bibliography.

This is a discussion of five main types of urban development systems, viewing the nature and control of urban land, the market regulation of urban development, statuatory planning control, the new town approach, and the leaseholder system.

Bahl, Roy W.; Campbell, Alan K.; and Greytak, David. TAXES EXPENDI-TURES, AND THE ECONOMIC BASE: CASE STUDY OF NEW YORK CITY. New York: Praeger, 1975. xxvi, 351 p. Index, pp. 346-51. Tables.

The five chapters of this report are devoted to the "Changes in the Structure of the New York City Economy," particularly changes in employment, income, population, and property value; "New York City Revenues and Economic Base," and the historical trends in these; "City Government Expenditures," containing a model developed to explain and forecast expenditures; "Employment, Real Wages and Work-load Increases;" and "The Fiscal and Income Distribution Effects of State Assumption."

Bartholomew, Harland. LAND USE IN AMERICAN CITIES. Cambridge, Mass.: Harvard University Press, 1955. vx, 196 p.

This book deals with the concept of planning and the active use of zoning in the growth and development of cities. Various types of cities are examined, as is the central city and its suburbs. Survey information from 86 cities over a 20-year period forms the basis for the analysis.

Bergsman, Joel; Greenston, Peter; and Healy, Robert. THE AGGLOMERATION PROCESS IN URBAN GROWTH. Washington, D.C.: Urban Institute, 1971. 37 p. No index.

This is the report of a study using cross-section data for 203 metro-politan areas in the United States in 1963. A cluster analysis was used to aggregate the 186 sectors for which data was gathered. The "Agglomerating Forces," "Methodology for Cluster Analysis," and "Results" are presented. An analysis remains to be done.

Berry, Brian J.L. METROPOLITAN AREA DEFINITION: A REEVALUATION OF CONCEPT AND STATISTICAL PRACTICE. Washington, D.C.: U.S. De-partment of Commerce, Bureau of the Census, 1968, revised 1969.

Birch, David [L.]; Atkinson, Reilly; and Linder, Sven Sandstrom. PATTERNS OF URBAN CHANGE: THE NEW HAVEN EXPERIENCE. Lexington, Mass.: Lexington Books, 1974. xviii, 163 p. Index, pp. 151-161. Maps, figures, tables.

This volume is the nontechnical companion to THE NEW HAVEN LABORATORY and is designed for the lay person interested in the dynamics of urban change and the functioning of urban areas. This is a report on the Harvard Business School project, looking at households, individuals, real estate, jobs, and patterns for the future in New Haven.

Bogue, Donald J. METROPOLITAN GROWTH AND THE CONVERSION OF LAND TO NON-AGRICULTURAL USES. Scripps Foundation Studies in Population Distribution. Scripps Foundation, 1956. 33 p.

This is an examination of metropolitan growth, city spread, major uses of land, land conversion and population growth. Other volumes in the Scripps Foundation Studies in Population Distribution are:

COMPARATIVE POPULATION AND URBAN RESEARCH VIA MULTI-PLE REGRESSION AND COVARIANCE ANALYSIS, by Donald J. Bogue and Dorothy L. Harris, 1954. vii, 75 p.

AN EXPLORATORY STUDY OF MIGRATION AND LABOR MOBIL-ITY USING SOCIAL SECURITY DATA, by Donald J. Bogue, 1950.

A METHODOLOGICAL STUDY OF MIGRATION AND LABOR MOBILITY IN MICHIGAN AND OHIO IN 1947, by Donald J. Bogue, 1952. vi, 100 p.

METROPOLITAN DECENTRALIZATION: A STUDY OF DIFFEREN-TIAL GROWTH, by Donald J. Bogue, 1950.

METROPOLITAN GROWTH AND THE CONVERSION OF LAND TO NONAGRICULTURAL USES, by Donald J. Bogue, 1956, 33 p.

MIGRATION WITHIN OHIO, 1935-40; A STUDY IN THE RE-DISTRIBUTION OF POPULATION, by Warren S. Thompson.

NEEDED URBAN AND METROPOLITAN RESEARCH, edited by Donald J. Bogue, 1953. x, 88 p.

SUBREGIONAL MIGRATION IN THE UNITED STATES, 1935-40, VOLUME 1, STREAMS OF MIGRATION (Joint with the Bureau of the Census, in preparation).

SUBREGIONAL MIGRATION IN THE UNITED STATES, 1935-40, VOLUME II, DIFFERENTIAL MIGRATION IN THE CORN AND COTTON BELTS, by Donald J. Bogue and Margaret Jarman Hagood, 1953. vi, 248 p.

SUBURBANIZATION OF MANUFACTURING ACTIVITY WITHIN STANDARD METROPOLITAN AREAS, by Evelyn M. Kitagawa and Donald J. Bogue, 1955. vi, 162 p.

SUBURBANIZATION OF SERVICE INDUSTRIES WITHIN STANDARD METROPOLITAN AREAS, by Ramond P. Cuzzort, 1955. vi, 71 p.

_____. POPULATION GROWTH IN SMAS 1900-1950 WITH AN EXPLANA-TORY ANALYSIS OF URBANIZED AREAS. Washington, D.C.: Government Printing Office, 1953. ix, 76 p.

This monograph was the first in a series of studies made for the Department of Commerce on the changing patterns of metropolitan growth. Census definition changes and growth trends in urban areas are included.

Broadbent, T.A. AN ATTEMPT TO APPLY MARX'S THEORY OF GROUND RENT TO THE MODERN URBAN ECONOMY. Research Paper no. 17. London: Center for Environmental Studies, 1975. 46 p.

Marx's rent analysis, which was largely agricultural in nature, is applied in the context of the modern city.

Castells, Manuel. THE URBAN QUESTION: A MARXIST APPROACH. Translated by Alan Sheridan. Cambridge: M.I.T. Press, 1977. x, 502 p. References, pp. 472-93. Index, pp. 493-502.

First published in French in 1972, the aim of this work is to "develop new tools of research while criticizing the traditional" (approaches). Castells calls for a critical revision of thinking among urban social scientists and for a rereading of the empirical discoveries. The book adapts Marxist concepts in its approach to urban theory. Major sections of the book include discussions of the historical process of urbanization, the urban ideology, the urban structure, urban politics, and the urban process.

Conroy, Michael E. THE CHALLENGE OF URBAN ECONOMIC DEVELOPMENT: GOALS, POSSIBILITIES, AND POLICIES FOR IMPROVING THE ECONOMIC STRUCTURE OF CITIES. Lexington, Mass.: Lexington Books, 1975. viii, 133 p. References, pp. 113-22. Index, pp. 123-33.

This book is designed as an introduction to urban policy. It is a synthesis of existing nontechnical work, and requires little knowledge of urban economics or urban geography. "A supplement and update of W. Thompson's Preface" if you will. Chapter headings are: (1) "Urban Growth U.S. Urban Economic Development," (2) "What Determines the Economic Structure of a City," (3) "What Determines the Level of Income in Urban Areas," (4) "Can Urban Income Stability be Improved," (5) "Issues in Urban Development," (6) "How Can the Development Prospects of an Area be Determined," and (7) "Research Needs in Urban Economic Development." Summaries conclude each chapter.

Cook, Gillian P. SPATIAL DYNAMICS OF BUSINESS GROWTH IN THE WATERSTRAND. Chicago: University of Chicago Department of Geography, 1975. x, 144 p. Bibliography, pp. 135-44. No index.

This is a work dealing with an urban study in South Africa which looks at metropolitan growth and the response of the business community to this growth. A model is developed, and information is set forth about the functioning of a particular metropolitan central business district.

Darin-Drabkin, H. LAND POLICY AND URBAN GROWTH. Urban and Regional Planning Series, vol. 16. Elmsford, N.Y.: Pergamon Press, 1977. 403 p. Index.

This is an account of land prices, various land policies, and the impact upon the urban environment. The market mechanism and government intervention are among the topics covered. There are a number of case studies, and the approach is analytical.

Duncan, Beverly, and Lieberson, Stanley. METROPOLIS AND REGION IN TRANSITION. Beverly Hills, Calif.: Sage Publications, 1970. 390 p. Bibliography, pp. 291-94. Index, pp. 295-301. Tables and figures.

A study was made in 1950 as a "midcentury benchmark," designed to document the state to which the metropolitan economy had evolved and to provide a baseline for subsequent change. In this work, the process of urbanization is discussed and documented by the establishment of economic bases and the development of metropolitan functions.

Duncan, Otis Dudley, et al. METROPOLIS AND REGION. Baltimore: Johns Hopkins Press for Resources for the Future, 1960. xviii, 587 p. Appendix of Data, pp. 551-60. Bibliography, pp. 561-76. Index, pp. 577-87.

Using data from a 1950 "mid-century" study of urban areas, the authors extensively describe and utilize the data in terms of theories of growth, location, and hierarchy. Part I examines "The Metropolitan Area and Its Functions," using location theory, economic base analysis, urban hierarchy, and major economic functions. Part II, "Metropolitan Dominance," uses examples from manufacturing and extractive industries in the hinterland to show urban dominance. Part III looks at "Industrial Structure and Regional Relationships." "50 Major Cities and their Regional Relations" are discussed in part IV.

Finkler, Earl, and Peterson, David L. NONGROWTH PLANNING STRATEGIES: THE DEVELOPING POWER OF TOWNS, CITIES AND REGIONS. New York: Praeger, 1974. xxv, 117 p. Bibliography, pp. 102-15.

In this volume, controlled and managed growth are discussed and contrasted to nongrowth. Social, environmental, and political issues, are dealt with. The economic and population effects of nongrowth are discussed. A case study in nongrowth (Boulder, Colo.) is presented.

Forrester, Jay W. URBAN DYNAMICS. Cambridge: M.I.T. Press, 1969. xiii, 298 p. Index, pp. 285.

Positive and negative feedback and systems dynamics are applied to urban growth in a "complex social system." A computerized simulation of the behavior of the system and reactions to changes in the system are included. Various policy alternatives may be included in the model.

Friedly, Philip H. NATIONAL POLICY RESPONSES TO URBAN GROWTH. Lexington, Mass.: Lexington Books, 1974. xv, 221 p. Index, pp. 219-21. Figures and tables.

This is a collection of the author's essays generated over a five-year period. There are sections in theory, policy, and practice

with five or six essays appearing in each section. Six appendixes
are included, giving, among other things, courses in regional
analysis and an annotated bibliography of African and Latin American related work.

Gottman, Jean. MEGALOPOLIS, THE URBANIZED NORTHEASTERN SEABOARD
OF THE UNITED STATES. New York: Twentieth Century Fund, 1961. xi,
810 p. Index.

The development of cities on the northeastern seaboard is examined
in detail. It traces the change from wilderness to the close suburbs
and deals with the "balances and counterforces," giving it (the
seaboard) unity.

Green, J.L. ECONOMIC ECOLOGY: BASELINES FOR URBAN DEVELOPMENT.
Athens: University of Georgia Press, 1969. xii, 169 p. Index.

The idea of a system within the context of urban development is
the theme of this book, with the reality of organizations and institutions integrated into an urban-industrial dynamics. A political-
economy approach is taken which examines transportation and housing in a development context.

Haig, Robert Murray. MAJOR ECONOMIC FACTORS IN METROPOLITAN
GROWTH AND ARRANGEMENT: A STUDY OF TRENDS AND TENDENCIES
IN THE ECONOMIC ACTIVITIES WITHIN THE REGION OF NEW YORK AND
ITS ENVIRONS. New York Regional Survey, 1927. New York: Regional
Plan of New York and Its Environs. xvii, 111 p. Index, pp. 109-11.

This is an analysis of a study of economic activities in the New
York City region. The studies relate to nine major industries.
Major discussions are of "Speculations Regarding Economic Bases of
Urban Concentration," "Assignment of Activities to Areas in Urban
Regions," and "Location Trends and Tendencies in New York and
Its Environs."

Hansen, Niles M. THE CHALLENGE OF URBAN GROWTH: THE BASIC ECO-
NOMICS OF CITY SIZE AND STRUCTURE. Lexington, Mass.: Lexington Books,
1975. xiv, 173 p. Notes, pp. 153-68. Index, pp. 169-73.

This is a study of the economics of urban growth and structure.
Issues which relate to alternative urban growth patterns and goal
choices are also discussed. The 12 chapters focus on "The Urban
System in the U.S.," "Where Do People Want to Live," "Some
Limitations of Economic Base and Other Models of Urban Growth,"
"Advantages of the City," "When Is A Big City Too Big," "The
Decline of the Central City," "The Central-City Neighborhood,"
"The Growth Controversy in the Suburbs," "Cluster Development,"
and "Urban Growth Center Policy and Regional Development."
The study is reasonably non-technical and designed for planners
in search of economic underpinnings.

_____. INTERMEDIATE SIZE CITIES AS GROWTH CENTERS: APPLICATIONS FOR KENTUCKY, THE PIEDMONT CRESCENT, THE OZARKS AND TEXAS. New York: Praeger, 1971. xv, 207 p. No index.

Growth center policy in the United States is considered in terms of rationale and specific applications. Chapter 1 sets the stage for the study by examining the "Problems of Metropolitan Growth." "Growth Center Theory," introduced in Chapter 2, deals with the French and non-French contributions to the body of theory. "Growth Center Experience in the United States and Abroad" is discussed in Chapter 3, and Chapter 4 looks at "Criteria for Growth Center Policy Revision." Chapters 5 through 8 examine specific cases in Kentucky, the Piedmont Crescent, the Ozarks, and South Texas. The book concludes with a discussion of "Migration, Housing, and the Costs of Growth."

_____. RURAL POVERTY AND THE URBAN CRISIS: A STRATEGY FOR REGIONAL DEVELOPMENT. Bloomington: Indiana University Press, 1970. xv, 352 p. Selected bibliography, pp. 313-23. Notes, pp. 324-48. Index, pp. 349-52.

This study began as a project designed to integrate urban and regional problems and programs into a "comprehensive and coherent framework for public policy purposes." A policy model is developed, and the approach links federal policy in depressed areas to the national problems of the urban crisis and unemployment. Specific chapters deal with "The National Setting," "The South," "Appalachia," "The Regional Commissions," "The Economic Development Administration," "The Indians," "The Mexican Americans," "The Industrialization of Rural America," "Urban Policy in a Mobile Society," and "Promoting Labor Mobility."

Harrison, Bennet. URBAN ECONOMIC DEVELOPMENT: SUBURBANIZATION, MINORITY OPPORTUNITY AND THE CONDITION OF THE CENTRAL CITY. Washington, D.C.: Urban Institute, 1974. xiv, 216 p. Index, pp. 201-16.

This book argues that the continuing "urban crisis" is a "failure of policy" in which central cities were written off too early. Harrison concludes that the central city is still a viable economic entity. Suggested reforms include capital deepening to aid central city development.

Hartwick, John, and Croroley, Ronald W. URBAN ECONOMIC GROWTH: THE CANADIAN CASE. Ottawa: Information Canada, 1972. xii, 402 p. Bibliography, pp. 398-401.

This study was designed to analyze the process of industrial and urban growth in Canada. It examines 46 cities and 67 industrial categories for 1951 and 1961. A model for urban growth is developed in the first chapter which incorporates micro theory and consumer behavior. The parameters of growth are then set forth, and the examination of Canadian cities is undertaken.

Hawley, Amos H. THE CHANGING SHAPE OF METROPOLITAN AMERICA: DECONCENTRATION SINCE 1920. Glencoe, Ill.: Free Press, 1956. 177 p. Appendix, pp. 170-74. Notes, pp. 175-77. No index.

This monograph charts the trend of the modern city, and society, in contrast to those of an earlier era. Population growth and redistribution in the United States are examined between 1900 and 1950. This includes looking at the distances from the central city, type of satellites, as well as geographical characteristics.

Henderson, J. Vernon. ECONOMIC THEORIES AND THE CITIES. New York: Academic Press, 1977. xi, 238 p. References, pp. 229-32. Index, pp. 233-38.

Modeling and urban land use models are discussed using technical investigations and economic theory. The first three chapters summarize the extent of urban land use models while chapters 4 through 10 apply and extend these basic models to study a wide range of urban problems ranging from externalities and housing to transportation.

Heroux, Richard L., and Wallace, William A. FINANCIAL ANALYSIS AND THE NEW COMMUNITY DEVELOPMENT PROCESS. New York: Praeger, 1973. x, 172 p.

Financial plans for new communities, methodology, models, and the land development process are topics included in this book. The basic argument is that for new towns to be viable, many factors, especially those which are economic in nature, must be considered. It is a strong plea for those people interested in the management of urban economic information.

Hoch, Irving. PROGRESS IN URBAN ECONOMICS: THE WORK OF THE COMMITTEE ON URBAN ECONOMICS 1959-1968, AND DEVELOPMENT OF THE FIELD. Washington, D.C.: Resources for the Future, 1969. xii, 132 p. Appendixes, pp. 29-132. Tables and figures.

An overview of urban economics is presented in the introductory discussion and is followed by several appendixes dealing with leading issues in the field, the evidence of growth and recognition of this field, doctorate programs in urban economics, and a history of the Committee on Urban Economics.

Hoover, Edgar M., and Vernon, Raymond. ANATOMY OF A METROPOLIS: THE CHANGING DISTRIBUTION OF PEOPLE AND JOBS WITHIN THE NEW YORK METROPOLITAN REGION. Cambridge: Harvard University Press, 1959. xvi, 345 p. Index, pp. 329-45.

Another of a series of books in the New York Metropolitan Study examining the forces shaping urban growth. Part I looks at "Cities and Suburbs." Part II examines "The Jobs," which includes discussions of "Location Pressures on Manufacturers," "The Special Manufacturing Industries," and "The White Collar Corporations." "The People" is the topic of part III. Ten appendixes deal with special aspects of the study and some data.

Hoyt, Homer. URBAN LAND USE REQUIREMENTS 1968-2000: THE LAND AREA REQUIRED FOR THE GROWTH OF THE URBAN POPULATION IN THE UNITED STATES DECEMBER 1968. Washington, D.C.: Homer Hoyt Inst., 1968, paper. iii, 34 p. No index.

Population projections for the year 2000 are used to estimate the need for urbanized land areas by that time. The monograph includes land use projections for several SMSAs.

James, Franklin J., and Hughes, James W. ECONOMIC GROWTH AND RESIDENTIAL PATTERNS: A METHODOLOGICAL INVESTIGATION. New Brunswick, N.J.: Rutgers University Press, 1972. 272 p.

Lapatra, Jack W. APPLYING THE SYSTEMS APPROACH TO URBAN DEVELOPMENT. New York: Dowden, Hutchinson and Ross, 1973. iv, 296 p. Bibliography, pp. 287-92. Index, pp. 293-96.

With a desire to promote problem solving in an increasingly complex urban environment, the author puts forth the capabilities and the promise of a systems approach. "The Systems Approach" is introduced, and models are developed and analyzed. There is also an application to regional analysis via location theory and location models.

Lewis, W. Cris, and Prescott, James R. URBAN-REGIONAL ECONOMIC GROWTH AND POLICY. Ann Arbor, Mich.: Ann Arbor Science Publishers, 1975. x, 220 p. Index, pp. 215-20.

A number of methodology and policy issues are considered using multiequation models, linear programming, multivariate statistics, regression analysis, and input-output techniques. The focus of this analysis is provided in chapters discussing "Development Concepts and Spatial Delineation," "Rural Community Development," "Labor Markets and Growth Centers," "Water Resource Development and Interregional Commodity Trade," "Metropolitan Planning and Inter-Urban Earnings Differentials," "State-Local Government and Regional Development Policies," and "Federal Policy: Experimental Cities and New Towns."

Louis, Edward Alfeld, and Graham, Alan K. INTRODUCTION TO URBAN DYNAMICS. Cambridge, Mass.: Wright-Allen Press, 1976. xvii, 337 p. Bibliography, pp. 331-33. Index, pp. 333-37. Illus.

Lowry, J.H. WORLD CITY GROWTH. London: Edward Arnold, 1975. 155 p.

Lund, Leonard. BUSINESS/GOVERNMENT PARTNERSHIP IN LOCAL ECO-
NOMIC DEVELOPMENT PLANNING. New York: Conference Board, 1976.
vi. 30 p. Bibliographic References.

McGraw, Eugene T., and Vernon, Thomas T. THE PROCESS OF URBANIZA-
TION: THE ECONOMIC ASPECTS. Manhattan: Kansas State University,
Center for Community Planning Service, 1977. 38 p.

Markusen, J.R., and Schaffman, D.T. SPECULATION AND MONOPOLY IN
URBAN DEVELOPMENT: ANALYTICAL FOUNDATIONS WITH EVIDENCE FOR
TORONTO. Toronto: University of Toronto Press, 1977. 176 p.

> A model of land development is developed which includes a theory
> of land pricing, giving special emphasis to market structure, specu-
> lation, and taxation. The case of Toronto is then set forth and
> tested. The book ends by discussing the role of government in
> land development policy.

Mills, Edwin S. STUDIES IN THE STRUCTURE OF THE URBAN ECONOMY.
Baltimore: Johns Hopkins University Press, 1972. xi, 151 p. References and
bibliography, pp. 143-45. Index, pp. 146-51.

> This book examines the questions how are cities organized and how
> is it that they change. An economic model is formulated to answer
> these questions and to provide a logical foundation for the analysis.
> Included are discussions of other trends and a survey of various
> urban models. Suggestions are also made for future research.

Mosely, Malcolm J. GROWTH CENTERS IN SPATIAL PLANNING. New York:
Pergamon Press, 1974. vii, 192 p. Bibliography, pp. 175-89. Index, pp. 189-92.

> This is a synthesis of the work in growth centers analysis to examine
> the spatial element of the world's problems. Urban centers, scale,
> agglomeration, and the impact of growth centers are discussed. The
> conclusion deals with implications for policy and research.

Neutze, [Grame] Max. AUSTRALIAN URBAN POLICY: OBJECTIVES AND
OPINIONS. Sidney: Allen and Unwin, 1978. 250 p.

> This is an integrated treatment of Australian urban policy. The
> author suggests that a wholistic treatment might lead to a more
> efficient use of resources and to improved equity between different
> groups of urban residents. This is especially useful for those in-
> terested in urban politics, town planning, urban economics, and
> political geography.

_____. ECONOMIC POLICY AND THE SIZE OF CITIES. Canberra: Aus-
tralian National University, 1965. xi, 136 p. Index, pp. 135-36.

> Neutze examines city growth in terms of its economic effects in

order to see if economic benefits are derived from either large or small centers. The aim is to determine if a policy of decentralization has economic viability. The work is largely theoretical with widespread applicability, though couched in an Australian context.

_____. "Economic Policy and the Solution of Australian Urban Problems." Paper presented to the Melbourne University Political Science Society. Warburton Chalet, August 1970. 12 p.

This is a discussion of segregation and income distribution in the context of economic policies for urban areas.

_____. URBAN DEVELOPMENT IN AUSTRALIA: A DESCRIPTIVE ANALYSIS. Sidney: George Allen and Unwin, 1977. 258 p. Bibliography, pp. 246-52. Index, pp. 253-58.

The intent of this book is to examine the way Australian cities have changed and to analyze both the structure and the functions of these cities. It is a book for policy makers and students of urban development who seek a descriptive analysis of urban change. Subjects covered range from the size distribution of cities to land use and transportation, housing, and the patterns of urban development. Summaries are found at the end of each chapter.

Ottensonann, John R. THE CHANGING SPATIAL STRUCTURE OF AMERICAN CITIES. Lexington, Mass.: Lexington Books, 1975. xiii, 207 p. Notes, pp. 187-200. Index, pp. 201-07. Figures and Tables.

A report on a longitudinal study in the Milwaukee urban area and in the United States. An examination is made of some relationships dealing with housing, population, employment, and transportation. Early chapters deal with the urban past and change in Milwaukee. The research approach is then set forth along with other urban models. The data set is available to other researchers.

Pfouts, Ralph W. THE TECHNIQUES OF URBAN ECONOMIC ANALYSIS. Trenton, N.J.: Chandler Davis Publishing Co., 1960. 410 p. No index.

This is an examination and critique of economic base theory with an explanation of the input-output alternatives. Part I elaborates the history, analysis, terminology, classification, and measurement of the economic base. Part II summarizes the objections to economic base theory with respect to classification errors in the base-ratios, empirical tests, and the community income multipliers. The alternative input-output approach is presented in part III.

Pittsburgh. Regional Planning Association. PORTRAIT OF A REGION. Economic Study of the Pittsburgh Region, vol. 2. Pittsburgh: University of Pittsburgh Press, 1963. xiv, 203 p. Notes, pp. 189-98. Index, pp. 199-203.

Ira Lowry was the major contributor in this volume, and in it he discusses the "Regional Framework" in its geographical setting and looks at the area as "A Place to Work" and "A Place to Live."

_____. REGION IN TRANSITION. Economic Study of the Pittsburgh Region, vol. 1. Pittsburgh: University of Pittsburgh Press, 1963. xxiv, 462 p. Notes, pp. 423-52. Index, pp. 452-62.

The four volumes in this series report the findings of a comprehensive study of the Pittsburgh area which took place in 1959. This first volume reports on the region itself, the employment patterns, wages, the business climate, the structure and growth of the region, transportation, fuels, metals, chemicals, industrial structure, and the administration of the area.

_____. REGION WITH A FUTURE. Economic Study of the Pittsburgh Region, vol. 3. Pittsburgh: University of Pittsburgh Press, 1963. xix, 313 p. Notes, pp. 290-304. Index, pp. 305-13.

This third volume of the Pittsburgh study examines Pittsburgh's relation to the national economy and its assets and liabilities. The prospects of key industries are viewed and the geographical shifts which are occurring within the region are noted.

_____. SUMMARY. Economic Study of the Pittsburgh Region, vol. 4. Pittsburgh: University of Pittsburgh Press, 1963.

Pred, Alan. CITY-SYSTEMS IN ADVANCED ECONOMIES: PAST GROWTH, PRESENT PROCESSES AND FUTURE DEVELOPMENT OPTIONS. New York: John Wiley and Sons, 1977. 256 p. Notes, pp. 218-30. References, pp. 231-48. Index, pp. 249-56. Maps and diagrams.

In the author's words, this book attempts "to provide answers to two questions. (1) What are the processes underlying...growth of post-industrial metropolitan complexes and (2) What are the implications of ongoing growth for efforts to reduce interregional inequalities of employment opportunities." While this book is of more interest to geographers, it provides interesting reading and information for regional and urban economists.

Ratcliff, Richard Updegraff. URBAN LAND ECONOMICS. New York: McGraw-Hill, 1949. xii, 533 p. Index, pp. 525-33.

The thesis of this work is that "the determination of urban land use is a market process." Land utilization patterns are examined and integrated into economic theory. Chapter 1 deals with the commodity traded--land rights. Chapters 2 through 5 look at demand factors in the urban land market, and chapters 6 and 7 look at the supply side. The remaining chapters explore urban finance, housing markets, city growth and structure, urban land policies, and housing policies.

Richardson, Harry W. THE ECONOMICS OF URBAN SIZE. Lexington, Mass.: D.C. Heath, 1973. vii, 243 p. Bibliography, pp. 215-32. Name Index, pp. 233-36. Subject Index, pp. 237-43.

This is a study which seeks to answer the question "Is big bad?" It is an attempt to see if city size is a factor in the urban crisis. Relationships between economic phenomena and city size are examined using economic theory and empirical data. Chapters include discussions of "The Theory of City Size," "Negative Externalities," "Economics and Agglomeration," "Income and Welfare," "Economic Structure," "Scale Economies in Local Government," "Market Tests and City Size," "Optimal City Size and Density," "Theory of Distribution of City Sizes," "City Size Distribution of City Sizes," "City Size Distributions: Empirical Aspects," "National Urban Size Policy," and "The Case of London."

_____. THE NEW URBAN ECONOMICS: AND ALTERNATIVES. London: Pion (distributed by Academic Press), 1977. 266 p. References, pp. 245-59. Name Index, pp. 260-62. Subject Index, pp. 263-66.

Richardson's monograph "surveys and discusses" the NUE and extends it with his own contributions. This provides a greater look at the theoretical underpinnings of urban economies. Chapter headings include: "What is New Urban Economics?" "Antecedents," "The Standard NUE Model," "Implications and Extensions of the Standard Model," "The Multicentric City," "More Complex Residential Location Patterns," "Locational Interdependence Towards Dynamics," "An Optimum Geography," "Two Residential Location Models," "Alternatives to NUE," "Political Economy," and "Conclusion: Are NUE Models Operational?"

Robson, Brian T. URBAN GROWTH: AN APPROACH. London: Methuen, 1973. xiv, 282 p. Index, pp. 268-82.

Historical data are presented as are theoretical concepts of urban growth and the process of urban growth. It is a statistical study of urban development using the rank size rules, systems analysis, and presenting an aggregate simulated model.

Rodwin, Lloyd. NATIONS AND CITIES: A COMPARISON OF STRATEGIES FOR URBAN GROWTH. Boston: Houghton-Mifflin, 1970. xvi, 395 p. Notes, pp. 293-365. Index, pp. 369-95.

This book deals with two problems which arise from alternative strategies to promote urban growth. They are: (1) the social costs of metropolitan growth centers, and (2) the disparity between growth centers and depressed areas. Case studies are used to amplify and test more general ideas on growth strategies and are developed in chapters 1 and 2. The remaining chapters examine strategies of Venezuela, Turkey, Great Britain, and France.

Rondinelli, Dennis A. URBAN AND REGIONAL DEVELOPMENT PLANNING: POLICY AND ADMINISTRATION. Ithaca, N.Y.: Cornell University Press, 1975. 272 p. Index, pp. 267-72.

First published in 1970, this book contains a heavy critique of U.S. planning theory and suggests the prescriptions are not adequate when applied to the complexities of urban areas.

Ross, C. George. THE URBANIZATION OF RURAL CALIFORNIA. Special Report no. 11. Berkeley, Calif.: Center for Real Estate and Urban Economics, Institute of Urban and Regional Development, 1975. xv, 223 p. Bibliography, pp. 188-94. Appendixes, pp. 195-23. No index.

This report closely examines the events surrounding the subdivision of recreational land in the state of California. A computer analysis is used to process information from a survey in 1973 and 1974.

Rust, Edgar. NO GROWTH: IMPACTS ON METROPOLITAN AREAS. Lexington, Mass.: D.C. Heath, 1975.

This volume examines the dynamics of non-growth in 10 SMSAs in the period between the 1940 and 1960. These are examined in their historical setting, in their more modern context, looking at population, migration, the quality of economic changes, age distributions, and the level of savings to consumption.

Schaffer, Richard Lance. INCOME FLOWS IN URBAN POVERTY AREAS: A COMPARISON OF THE COMMUNITY INCOME ACCOUNTS OF BEDFORD-STUYVESANT. Lexington, Mass.: Lexington Books, 1973. 110 p.

Shafer, Thomas W. URBAN GROWTH AND ECONOMICS. Reston, Va.: Reston Publishing Co., 1977. xv, 233 p. Bibliography, pp. 205-09. Index, pp. 231-33.

This book approaches urban growth with the questions: why cities exist, why they are located where they are, and why they grow. Part 1 is essentially historical, and parts 2 and 3 deal with growth. Part 4 examines the role of government and other institutions in urban areas.

Smith, Peter, and Morrison, W.I. SIMULATING THE URBAN ECONOMY: EXPERIMENTS WITH INPUT-OUTPUT TECHNIQUES. Monographs in Spatial and Environmental Systems Analysis #7. London: Pion (Distributed by Academic Press, N.Y.), 1974. 151 p. References, pp. 84-88. Author Index, pp. 149-50. Subject Index, p. 151.

A discussion, review, and evaluation of I-O techniques and the results of an empirical study of Peterborough using both survey and nonsurvey data. The technical coefficient from these two data-sources are critically compared, and suggestions are made for the improvement of nonsurvey methods.

Smith, Walace F. URBAN DEVELOPMENT: THE PROCESS AND THE PROBLEMS. Berkeley and Los Angeles: University of California Press, 1975. xvii, 381 p. Index, pp. 375-81.

This is a comprehensive view of the complex interlocking system within cities involving landowners, developers, investors, planners, and government officials. The decisions made which shape urban areas are set into the context of location theory, property rights, financial institutions, technology, consumer preferences, and so on. Annotated selected references are included at the end of each of the 15 chapters.

Spiegelman, Robert S. ANALYSIS OF URBAN AGGLOMERATION AND ITS MEANING FOR RURAL PEOPLE. Washington, D.C.: Economic Research Service, U.S. Department of Agriculture, June 1966. 24 p. Selected Bibliography, pp. 19-24.

A monograph for researchers that looks at agglomeration literature and explores theories of agglomeration. Suggestions for future research are also included, with the major focus centering on approaches to rural poverty.

Rybeck, Walter. PROPERTY TAXATION AND URBAN GROWTH. Washington, D.C.: Urban Institute, 1970. 72 p.

This is a summary of a seminar on the economics, politics, and problems of property tax issues using metropolitan Washington, D.C., as an example.

Tomlinson, Ralph. URBAN STRUCTURE: THE SOCIAL AND SPATIAL CHARACTER OF CITIES. New York: Random House, 1969. xv. 335 p.

This is a study of urban sociology and ecology, part 2 of which is devoted to location theory, the economic base, and central place theory. Economic and social forces which shape cities are examined.

Ullman, Edward L.; Dacey, Michael F.; and Brodsky, Harold. THE ECONOMIC BASE OF AMERICAN CITIES: PROFILES FOR THE 101 METROPOLITAN AREAS OVER 250,000 POPULATION BASED ON MINIMUM REQUIREMENTS FOR 1960. Seattle: University of Washington Press, 1971. 118 p. No index.

This report discusses the minimum requirements technique which was devised by Ullman and Dacey as a short cut for calculating the ratio of export to internal employment. The report deals with the "Economic Base of Cities," the "Minimum Requirements for 1960," and "Minimum Requirements Compared to Other Surveys." Appendixes are devoted to "Characteristics of 101 U.S. Metropolitan Areas over 250,000 Population, 1960," "Export-Internal Employment Stockholm, Sweden, 1950, Based on American Minima," and "The Minimum Requirements Approach to the Urban Economic Base."

U.S. Advisory Commission on Interregional Government Relations. URBAN AND RURAL AMERICA: POLICIES FOR FUTURE GROWTH. Washington, D.C.: 1968. xvi, 186 p.

This report was written to respond to questions about new communities and the future growth of urban areas. State and local regulations, plans, and considerations are viewed in the context of urbanization.

Vietorisy, Thomas, and Harrison, Bennett. THE ECONOMIC DEVELOPMENT OF HARLEM. New York: Lowdon Preger, 1970. xxv, 287 p. Appendixes. No index.

This book reports on a one-year field study in Harlem and discusses "A Profile of the Harlem Economy," "The Need for Ghetto Development," "The Problems of Project Selection," "The Support and Upgrading of Existing Enterprises," "Recommended Development Projects," and "Interfacing Harlem Development with the Growth of the New York City Economy."

Von Eckardt, Wolf. THE CHALLENGE OF MEGALOPOLIS. New York: Macmillan Co., 1964. 128 p. Index, pp. 126-8. Maps. Illus.

This is a somewhat condensed version of J. Gottman's MEGALOPOLIS (see p. 22) which sets forth some of the central findings of that work. It is presented here in nontechnical language. Chapter headings include: "Megalopolis: A Very Special Region," "The Economic Hinge," "Why Cities Grow and Suburbs Scatter," "The Revolution in Land Use," "Earning a Living Intensely," "The Job Revolution," "Transportation," "Living and Working Together," and "The Challenge of Megalopolis."

Washnis, George J. COMMUNITY DEVELOPMENT STRATEGIES: CASE STUDIES OF MAJOR MODEL CITIES. New York: Praeger, 1974. 400 p. Index. Tables and charts.

This is a summary of the experiences of Boston, Chicago, Dayton, Indianapolis, New York, Newark, Savannah, and Seattle and how the model cities program became a broad based community development program.

Wheat, Leonard. URBAN GROWTH IN THE NONMETROPOLITAN SOUTH. Lexington, Mass.: Lexington Books, 1976. xvi, 173 p. Index, pp. 169-173.

This is a cross-sectional statistical analysis which avoids the limitations of city data and examines most of the more popular hypothesis which seeks to explain why some nonmetropolitan areas grow (faster than others). A sample of 116 southern cities is used, and the study is designed to control several factors which often bias findings. The methodology is elaborated as are the sectors within the model. An appendix gives predictions for future growth.

Wibberly, G. AGRICULTURE AND URBAN GROWTH: A STUDY OF COM-
PETITION FOR RURAL LAND. London: M. Joseph, 1959.

Wilhelm, Paul, and Torrone, Robert. URBAN GROWTH. Rochelle Park, N.J.:
Hayden Book Co., 1975. 149 p. Index, pp. 147-49.

    A high school text which looks at specific issues and problems of
U.S. cities. Chapter 10 lists "Resources and Activities," including books, filmstrips, simulations, and cassette tapes.

Wright, Ivan, and Wolkiser, Arthur M. THE ECONOMIC BASE OF THE
WEALTH AND WELFARE OF NEW YORK CITY. New York: Brooklyn College
Press, 1943. iv, 73 p. Paper.

    A collection of materials for use in "city economics" courses. It
is mostly a wealth, management, and budget analysis of New York
City.

Yuill, Robert S. A GENERAL MODEL FOR URBAN GROWTH: A SPATIAL
SIMULATION. Ann Arbor: Department of Geography, University of Michigan,
1970. 221 p. Bibliography, pp. 206-21. No index.

    This is an examination of the spatial patterns and processes which
contribute to economic growth. Chapters deal specifically with
the "Development of the Simulation Model," the "Input Parameters
of the Model," the "Simulated Growth of Actual Cities," and an
"Evaluation and Implications of the Model."

Chapter 4
URBAN PLANNING AND POLICY

Abouchar, Alan. EFFICIENCY IN THE URBAN ECONOMY. Toronto: Institute for Quantitative Analysis of Social and Economic Policy, University of Toronto, 1974. 56 p. Bibliography, pp. 55-56. (Illus.)

Bebout, John E., and Grele, Ronald J. WHERE CITIES MEET: THE URBANIZATION OF NEW JERSEY. Princeton, N.J.: D. Van Nostrand Company, 1964. xiii, 143 p. Index, pp. 129-43.

> This is a historical and current view of a part of megalopolis that examines the population, geographic, and economic growth of urban New Jersey.

Bor, Walter. THE MAKING OF CITIES. London: Leonard Hill, 1972. xiii, 269 p.

> This is a balanced look at planning and urban problems in the United States and United Kingdom for the layman. Among the topics covered are the growth and decay of the city and region, the political framework, housing, and transportation in urban life.

Broadbent, Thomas Andrew. PLANNING AND PROFIT IN THE URBAN ECONOMY. London: Methuen, 1970. xiv, 274 p. Bibliography, pp. 251-65. Index, pp. 266-74. Diagrams, graphs, and maps.

> Broadbent classifies this as an essay, not a piece of research, in which he puts many different urban-related topics together in a "wider context." There are numerous uses of economic and regional tools. The book begins with a discussion of the U.K. as an "overdeveloped economy." Here Broadbent discusses economic growth and its effects at an urban level. In chapter 2, "The State: Short Term Myopia and the Chief Stick," mainstream economics is integrated. Chapter 3 deals with "The Urban System: Labor and Production," while chapter 4 looks at "The Local State," with discussions of urban government and urban planning. Chapter 5 lays out "Current Theories of Urban Development" and integrates discussions of conventional economic theory, spatial theory, plural-

ism, and "ultra radical" models. "Planning Practice" and a conclusion end Broadbent's essay.

Clawson, Marion, and Hall, Peter. PLANNING AND URBAN GROWTH: AN
ANGLO-AMERICAN COMPARISON. Baltimore: Johns Hopkins University
Press for Resources for the Future, 1973. vii, 300 p. Index, pp. 289-300.
Tables and figures.

> This is the "capstone" of two major research efforts on planning
> and urban policy, drawing heavily from the two books of those
> efforts. (PLANNING AND ECONOMIC POLICY and POLICY
> AND ECONOMIC PLANNING). It offers an overview of urban
> economic growth and the planning process. There is a minimum
> of detailed analysis and more summation, general relations, inter-
> polations, and conclusions. The book generates a pre- and post-
> World War II comparison of urbanization in the United States and
> United Kingdom. The areas of planning, land use, and new towns
> are examined for use in the future based on past experiences.

Committee for Economic Development. AN APPROACH TO FEDERAL URBAN
POLICY. New York: 1977. 60 p.

> This is a policy statement by the CED which advocates more
> flexible approaches of federal urban policy due to the diverse
> needs of each urban area.

_____. GUIDING METROPOLITAN GROWTH. Washington, D.C.: Govern-
ment Printing Office, 1960. 55 p.

> This is a review of the growth process and the problems of urban
> areas. Particular emphasis is given to government involvement in
> these problems. Recommendations for the future include base
> studies, reorganization of government structures to plan and bud-
> get, and a renewal of business leadership in the growth process.

Connecticut University. School of Business Administration. Center for Real
Estate and Urban Economic Studies. EMPLOYMENT AND INDUSTRIAL DEVELOP-
MENT. Storrs: 1974. viii, 67 p. Bibliography. No index.

> This volume contains essays by W. Thompson, W. Kennard, and
> S. Messner.

Connery, Robert H., and Leach, Richard H. THE FEDERAL GOVERNMENT
AND METROPOLITAN AREAS. Cambridge: Harvard University Press, 1960.
x, 275 p. Bibliographical Note, pp. 239-43. Notes, pp. 243-62. Index,
pp. 263-75.

> This is the report of a nationwide study of government problems
> and activities in metropolitan areas by a group of scholars appoint-
> ed by the American Political Science Association. Topic areas

covered include: "Federal Programs in Metropolitan Areas," "Congress and Metropolitan Areas," "A Department of Urban Affairs: Pro and Con," "A Case for Federal Action," and "Recommendations."

Coppard, Larry C., and Goodman, Frederick L., eds. URBAN GAMING/SIMULATION '77. Ann Arbor: School of Education, University of Michigan, 1977. Index. Bibliography.

Current information on the "state of the art" is provided with an overview of the field, 65 sections about specific urban games, and a bibliography. Lots of games are included, most of which are not economic in nature.

Cullingworth, J.B. PROBLEMS OF AN URBAN SOCIETY. Vol. 1: THE SOCIAL FRAMEWORK OF PLANNING. Toronto: University of Toronto Press, 1973. 194 p.

The problems in urban areas which are created by social and economic change are examined in this and the two companion volumes written by Cullingworth. The focus of the first volume is on the changing demographic, social and economic structure, land shortages, and transportation needs of a technical-urban society.

_____. PROBLEMS OF AN URBAN SOCIETY. Vol. 2: THE SOCIAL CONTENT OF PLANNING. Toronto: University of Toronto Press, 1973. 191 p.

Urban poverty, disadvantage, and the lack of command over, or access to, resources in urban areas are the focuses of this second volume of PROBLEMS OF AN URBAN SOCIETY. Issues and the lack of a political base are stressed.

_____, ed. PROBLEMS OF AN URBAN SOCIETY. Vol. 3: PLANNING FOR CHANGE. Toronto: University of Toronto Press, 1973. 195 p.

This volume consists of papers which examine current urban problems. Multidisciplinary approaches to planning and the future of urban areas are examined.

deTorres, Juan. ECONOMIC DIMENSIONS OF MAJOR METROPOLITAN AREAS: POPULATION, HOUSING, EMPLOYMENT AND INCOME. New York: National Industrial Conference Board, 1968. iv, 52 p. Glossary, pp. 49-51. Bibliography, p. 52.

Topics reviewed in this monograph include the "Data and Coverage," "Population and Housing," "Employment and Income," and "Basic Data: Statistical Tables."

Downs, Anthony. URBAN PROBLEMS AND PROSPECTS. Chicago: Markham Publishing Co., 1970. 293 p. No index.

Downs includes essays on a wide variety of alternatives for current urban problems. He focuses on institutional changes within the economic and technological framework in such areas as growth, racism, the poor, schools, and land values. The 11 essays include: "Alternative Forms of Future Urban Growth in the U.S.," "Alternative Futures for the American Ghetto," "Racism in America and How to Combat It," "Moving Toward Realistic Housing Goals," "Home Ownership and American Free Enterprise," "Housing the Urban Poor: The Economics of Various Strategies," "The Law of Peak-Hour Expressway Congestion."

Flax, Michael J. A STUDY IN COMPARATIVE URBAN INDICATORS: CONDITIONS IN 18 LARGE METROPOLITAN AREAS. Washington, D.C.: Urban Institute, 1972. xii, 144 p. Exhibits and tables.

The ongoing program at the Urban Institute studying urban indicators has produced this report for government administrators, planners, businesses, labor, and the like to provide (a) a methodology for quantitatively presenting urban conditions and (b) to provide benchmarks on the quality of life in these selected areas.

Forstall, Richard, and Jones, Victor. SELECTED DEMOGRAPHIC, ECONOMIC, AND GOVERNMENTAL ASPECTS OF THE CONTEMPORARY METROPOLIS. Toronto: Centennial Study and Training Program of Metropolitan Research, Bureau of Municipal Research, July 1967. ix, 83 p. Tables.

This is an account and findings of a study of urban areas with populations of 100,000 or over which examined urban growth, function, and the framework of administrative areas. An appendix discusses "The Delimitation of Metropolitan Areas."

Greer, Scott. THE URBAN VIEW: LIFE AND POLITICS IN METROPOLITAN AMERICA. New York: Oxford University Press, 1972. 355 p.

This collection of essays examines the urban area from the "inside" looking out. The wealth, employment, talent, and troubles are dealt with at an introductory level. Urban futures and the urban past are examined.

Haig, Robert Murray. TOWARDS UNDERSTANDING THE METROPOLIS. Parts 1 and 2. New York: Arno Press, 1976. pp. 179-218; 402-34.

These are reprints of two QJE articles first published in February and May of 1926. Included are discussions of the economic base of an urban area and the activities of these areas. It summarizes trends in location found in an early study of New York City.

Holleb, Doris B. SOCIAL AND ECONOMIC INFORMATION FOR URBAN PLANNING: ITS SELECTION AND USE. Vol. 1. Chicago: University of Chicago, Center for Urban Studies, 1969. xxiii, 210 p. Index, pp. 187-210.

An in-depth examination of the ways to extract relevant information from urban data is presented in this monograph. Sections also detail ways to assemble this information for better use.

House, Peter. THE URBAN ENVIRONMENTAL SYSTEM: MODELING FOR RESEARCH POLICY MAKING AND EDUCATION. Beverly Hills, Calif.: Sage Publications, 1973. 316 p. Notes, pp. 263-66. References, pp. 267-82. Figures and tables.

The model is the focus of this book. It is a general environmental model which is flexible enough for use in a metropolitan or a regional setting.

Hughs, James W. URBAN INDICATORS, METROPOLITAN EVOLUTION AND PUBLIC POLICY. New Brunswick, N.J.: Rutgers University Press, 1973. 232 p. Bibliography, pp. 228-32. No Index.

Residential social patterns of cities are summarized and a system of urban social indicators is developed in this book by using a factor-analytic model. A test of the model is made using residential differentiation in North American cities. Major sections are devoted to the "Analysis of Urban Spatial Structure," "Factors, Structure and Urban Indicators," and "Metropolitan Evolution and Public Policy."

Ingram, Gregory K.; Kain, John F.; and Ginn, J. Royce. DETROIT PROTO-TYPE OF THE NBER URBAN SIMULATION MODEL. New York: National Bureau of Economic Research, 1972. xix, 233 p. Bibliography, pp. 225-28. Index, pp. 229-33. Figures, tables, and exhibits.

This volume details the ins and outs of the NBER model, discussing the theoretical issues involved as well as the practical alternatives. Also highlighted is the modeling process, including submodels and modeling in the housing market. The intent of the NBER model was to synthesize and extend both the analytical and theoretical understanding of urban growth and development. This is a report on the first phase of its application.

Leven, Charles L. THEORY AND METHOD OF INCOME AND PRODUCT ACCOUNTS FOR METROPOLITAN AREAS, INCLUDING THE ELGIN-DUNDEE AREA AS A CASE STUDY. Ann Arbor, Mich.: University Microfilms, 1958. vi, 292 p. Bibliography, pp. 245-250. No index.

The purpose of Leven's dissertation is to "devise a set of income and product accounts appropriate for economic analysis at the metropolitan level and then to estimate these for a specific pilot area." The work is divided into three parts. The first, "Theory," contains examinations of "Multiplier Analysis, Economic Structure and Social Activity," "The Sectors of Metropolitan Area Activity," and "Income and Product Accounts for Metropolitan Area." Part

II, "Method," looks at "The Empirical Requirements of the Accounts," "The Elgin-Dundee Area," and a "Description of Survey Research used in Estimating the Accounts." Part III generates the "Results and Conclusions" of the study, the "Incorporation of Survey Results into the Accounts," and the "Income and Product Accounts for the Elgin-Dundee Area."

McFarland, M. Carter. FEDERAL GOVERNMENT AND URBAN PROBLEMS, HUD: SUCCESSES, FAILURE AND THE FATE OF OUR CITIES. Boulder, Colo.: Westview Press, 1978. xviii, 277 p. Notes, pp. 251-66. Index, pp. 267-77.

This book takes a critical look at the programs and performance of HUD and suggests ways for future improvement. The 14 chapters deal with urban renewal, housing, urban research, financing housing construction, and the impediments to urban improvement.

McKenzie, R.D. THE METROPOLITAN COMMUNITY. New York: McGraw-Hill, 1933. xi, 352 p. Index, pp. 345-52.

This monograph was prepared as part of a series examining recent social trends in the United States for the President's Research Committee on Social Trends. The book is divided into five parts, and there are a number of divisions within each part. Part I considers "Recent Trends in Population Distribution" (particularly urban aggregation). Part II deals with "The Rise of the Metropolitan Community." Part III explores the "Interrelations of Cities," and part IV covers "The Process of Metropolitan Expansion." "Problems of the Large City" are explored in the final part. A lengthy appendix of urban related census data is included at the end.

Oakland Task Force. FEDERAL DECISION MAKING AND IMPACT IN URBAN AREAS: A STUDY OF OAKLAND. New York: Praeger, 1970. v, 216 p., and xcv. Bibliography. Tables.

After the riots of the 60s, this task force began to examine Oakland's problems, the federal response to those problems, the impact of these programs, and the strategies involved. This is the report of that task force.

Oberman, Joseph. PLANNING AND MANAGING THE ECONOMY OF THE CITY: POLICY GUIDELINES FOR THE METROPOLITAN MAYOR. New York: Praeger, 1972. xxii, 355 p.

Economic development is seen as a necessary concern of local government, and the process is seen as needing a sound data base and careful examination. The work was based on the Philadelphia Economic Development Unit, and many examples are from this study. "Data Banks and Measurements," "Financing the Metropolis," "Toward More Comprehensive Economic Growth Indicators,"

"Capital Formation," and "A Program for the Future" are a few titles of the book's eight chapters.

Pettingill, Robert, and Uppal, J.S. CAN CITIES SURVIVE? A STUDY OF SOME URBAN FISCAL PROBLEMS. New York: St. Martin's Press, 1974.

This is a discussion of the major urban fiscal problems and the unequal balance between cities and suburbs. Comparative studies of city's expenditures, revenue, and the gap between revenue and income are presented.

Speare, Alden Jr.; Goldstein, Sidney; and Frey, William H. RESIDENTIAL MOBILITY, MIGRATION AND METROPOLITAN CHANGE. Cambridge, Mass.: Ballinger Publishing Co., 1974. xvi, 316 p. Bibliography, pp. 229-308. Index, pp. 309-16.

This book reports on a case study of urban growth and decline which is occurring with greater frequency, the decline of the central city, and the rise of outlying areas. The authors compared social, economic, and demographic correlates for the urban areas in Rhode Island. Chapters include: "Population and Economic Change in Rhode Island," "Correlates of Population Redistribution and Migration," "The Declining Central City," "Area Determinants of Residential Mobility," "Individual and Household Determinants of Mobility," and "The Theory of Geographical Mobility."

Stanback, Thomas M., Jr., and Knight, Richard V. THE METROPOLITAN ECONOMY: THE PROCESS OF EMPLOYMENT EXPANSION. New York: Columbia University Press, 1970. xxi, 279 p. Index, pp. 271-79.

This is a study of the dynamics of employment expansion in the United States with emphasis on the metropolitan labor market, the dynamics of growth with respect to 32 industries, and the correlation of the metropolitan labor market with other sectors. Data was used from the 1940, 1950, and 1960 censuses and organized for 368 labor markets according to size and dominant economic function. Substantive findings include the varying growth rates of different sized cities.

Turnnard, Christopher. THE MODERN AMERICAN CITY. Princeton, N.J.: D. Van Nostrand Co., 1969. 192 p. Further reading, pp. 185-87. Index, pp. 187-92.

This is a view of the "dynamics of the American City." The second part of the book contains readings on urban agglomerations, forecasting, and cities "in trouble."

U.S. Advisory Commission on Intergovernmental Relations. DIRECTORY OF FEDERAL STATISTICS FOR METROPOLITAN AREAS. Washington, D.C.: Government Printing Office, 1962. 83 p.

U.S. Bureau of the Budget. STANDARD METROPOLITAN STATISTICAL AREAS. Washington, D.C.: Government Printing Office, 1974. 56 p. Maps.

This is an alphabetical listing of each SMSA by county definition and population.

U.S. Department of Housing and Urban Development. National Research Council. A STRATEGIC APPROACH TO URBAN RESEARCH AND DEVELOPMENT: SOCIAL AND BEHAVIORAL CONSIDERATIONS. Washington, D.C.: National Academy of Science, 1969. 100 p.

Long range research and development programs for the current and future needs of the nation's urban areas are discussed by participants from all of the social sciences. The focus is on the social, economic, and institutional factors and the development of alternative strategies to deal with urban issues.

Vernon, Raymond. METROPOLIS 1985: AN INTERPRETATION OF THE FINDINGS OF THE NEW YORK METROPOLITAN REGION STUDY. Cambridge, Mass.: Harvard University Press, 1960. xiii, 252 p. Notes, pp. 241-44. Index, pp. 245-52.

This book is the by-product of a series of books which examine "the forces which shape metropolitan America." This is a interpretation of the findings of that series, and it has applicability to studies in urban economic development and regional planning. Chapters include: "The Metropolis Today," "Origins of a Metropolitan Region," "Growth in the Region's Industries," Labor and Freight," "External Economies," "From Jobs to People to Jobs Again," "The Distribution of Jobs Within the Region," "Jobs in Motion," "From Tenement to Split Level," "City Hall and Town Hall," and "Metropolis 1985."

Weber, Max. THE CITY. Translated and edited by Don Martindale and Gertrud Neuworth. Glencoe, Ill.: Free Press, 1958. 242 p. Selective Bibliography, pp. 231-32. Index, pp. 233-42.

Weber's focus on the city is a historical one dating from ancient cities forward. Within this context, Weber examines the theory, the nature, the types, and the economic structures of cities.

Wilsher, Peter, and Righter, Rosemary. THE EXPLODING CITIES. New York: Quadrangle, New York Times Book Co., 1975. 238 p. Bibliography, pp. 225-31. Index, pp. 231-38.

This is a world view of the metropolitan growth of the 1970s and predicted growth in the future. Urban agglomerations are examined in light of "The Explosive Ingredients," "The Crisis of Affluence," "Cities of the Poor," and "Communes and Communism."

Zisch, William E.; Douglas, Paul H.; and Weaver, Robert C. THE URBAN ENVIRONMENT, HOW IT CAN BE IMPROVED. New York: New York University Press, 1969. xx, 107 p.

Urban problems such as poverty, transportation, and education are brought together and discussed at a national level. Views of how business and government can help alleviate the "crisis" are put forth with job creation, housing, and investment as primary priorities in solving these problems.

Chapter 5
URBAN PROBLEMS, LAND USE, AND SUBURBS

Ash, Maurice. REGIONS OF TOMORROW: TOWARDS THE OPEN CITY.
New York: Shocken Books, 1969. vii, 99 p. Bibliography, pp. 95-98. Index, p. 99.

Ash classifies this book as having the risk of being antiacademic.
It is not written for scholars, yet the philosophy underlying the
discussion is of a scholarly nature. Among other topics, "The
Disolution of Hierarchy," "Social Science, Form and Planning,"
and "The Anatomy of City-Regions," are examined.

Bell, Carolyn Shaw. THE ECONOMICS OF THE GHETTO. New York:
Pegasus, 1970. 267 p. Notes, pp. 241-52. Appendix, pp. 253-54. Bibliography, pp. 255-62. Index, pp. 263-67.

This book originated in a research seminar and its ten chapters
discuss: "The Economy and the Ghetto," "Income and Poverty,"
"Housing," "The Economics of People," "Employment and the
Labor Market," "Consumers and Markets," "Income and Welfare
Programs," "Employment and Training," "Education and Housing,"
and "The Ghetto Economy."

Berry, Brian J.L., and Kasarda, John D. CONTEMPORARY URBAN ECOLOGY.
New York: Macmillan Co., 1977. xiii, 497 p. References, pp. 430-76.
Author Index, pp. 477-80. Subject Index, pp. 481-97.

This is an interdisciplinary approach to urban issues. Current
problems and issues are stressed. Designed for upper level and
graduate courses in urban studies and the like, it could be supple-
mented for use in economics. Organizational divisions are: social construction of local communities; intraurban form and structure, metropolitan expansion and structural change; regional growth,
and urban systems, comparative urban structure, and planned change.

Berry, Brian J.L., et al. LAND USE, URBAN FORM AND ENVIRONMENTAL
QUALITY. Chicago: University of Chicago, Department of Geography, 1974.
xxiii, 440 p. Literature Cited, pp. 431-40. No index.

This is a report of a study at the University of Chicago for the office of Research and Development of the U.S. Environmental Protection Agency. The study deals with the ways in which urban form and land use affect the nature and intensity of environmental pollution from one urban area to another and within an urban area itself. An underlying aspect of this analysis is the question of the adoption of a national land use policy which will affect urban futures in a very direct way.

Birch, David L. THE ECONOMIC FUTURE OF CITY AND SUBURB. New York: Committee for Economic Development, 1970. xii, 41 p. No index.

Birch looks at the disadvantages of cities in terms of space costs, transportation costs, and taxes and examines the tremendous concentration of economic activity that is found there. He stresses the increasing specialization that is to be found in cities in the service sector. In examining other factors, he concludes that the central city is no longer able to function as a "general-purpose economic system." In viewing "The Changing Economic Function," Birch deals with "The City's Increasing Specialization," "The Suburb Versus the City," and "The Life Cycle of the City." In turning to "The Changing Residential Function," he examines growth patterns, age, income, and mobility.

Carey, George W.; Lober, Leonard; Greenberg, Michael; and Hordon, Robert. URBANIZATION, WATER POLLUTION, AND PUBLIC POLICY. New Brunswick, N.J.: Rutgers University Press, 1972. 214 p. Bibliography.

A mathematical model is used to relate urban growth to water pollution in the New York-New Jersey metropolitan area. Major sections of the book include discussions and analysis relating to: "The Present State of the Regional Hydrological System" and "Toward a Policy-Oriented Statistical Model for Estimating the Probable Future State of the Regions' Rivers."

Cooper, James R., and Guntermann, Karl L. REAL ESTATE AND URBAN LAND ANALYSIS. Lexington, Mass.: Lexington Books, 1973. 544 p. Figures, tables, bibliography.

This book gives an approach to the decision making process in real estate markets in the "underlying process of city growth and change which build, create, and destroy land values" in urban areas. The eight parts of the book contain examinations of "Urban Growth," "Urban Structure," "Urban Problems," "The Legal Environment of Urban Space Use," "Housing," "Urban Redevelopment," "Valuation and Investment Analysis," and "Large-Scale Real Estate Development."

Costello, V.F. URBANIZATION IN THE MIDDLE EAST. Cambridge, Mass.: Cambridge University Press, 1977. viii, 121 p. Appendix, pp. 111-13. References Cited, pp. 114-18. Index, pp. 119-21.

Designed for undergraduates studying social change, this book examines the life of a traditional Middle East city which has been transformed by modern technology. The environment, society, preindustrial urban society, rural-urban migration, modern urban development, and urban form and structure are among the topics discussed.

Derthick, Martha. NEW TOWNS IN TOWN: WHY A FEDERAL PROGRAM FAILED. Washington, D.C.: Urban Institute, 1972. xv, 103 p. Glossary of Annonyms, p. 103. No index.

This is an analysis of seven federal projects funded during the Johnson administration, none of which had more than minimum success. The "Program Origins and Objectives" are discussed as are the individual projects in Washington, D.C., San Antonio, Atlanta, New Bedford, San Francisco, Clinton Twp., and a program in Louisiana. A "Post Mortem" is included.

Dorau, Herbert, and Hinman, Albert. URBAN LAND ECONOMICS. New York: Macmillan Co., 1928. xvi, 570 p. Reprint. College Park, Md.: McGrath Publishing Co., 1969. Index.

This is an early text on urban land development which bases its approach on the work of Richard T. Ely.

Downs, Anthony. FEDERAL HOUSING SUBSIDIES: HOW ARE THEY WORKING? Lexington, Mass.: Lexington Books, 1973. 160 p.

This report to several banking and building associations concludes that poverty is the major cause of housing problems. Recommendations are made for future action.

_____. OPENING UP THE SUBURBS: URBAN STRATEGY FOR AMERICA. New Haven, Conn.: Yale University Press, 1973. ix, 319 p. No index.

Compiled after a series of six lectures dealing with suburban-dominated urban growth in the United States, Downs includes discussions on the decline of the central city and the ways of dealing with its plight. Costs and benefits of reform and the possibility of economically balanced population through incentives are dealt with, and various proposed strategies are examined along with the arguments surrounding each of them.

Dwyer, D.J. THE CITY IN THE THIRD WORLD. New York: Harper and Row, 1974. 280 p.

This is an examination of the urbanization process in the developing nations and the problems which have resulted. Comparisons are made between the urbanization process in industrialized and in developing countries.

EDITORIAL RESEARCH REPORT ON THE URBAN ENVIRONMENT. Washington, D.C.: Congressional Quarterly, 1969.

These are essays dealing with topics ranging from demography to violence and welfare to new towns in the urban setting. Particular emphasis is placed on the future and the "challenges" which must be met.

Evans, Hazel, ed. NEW TOWNS: THE BRITISH EXPERIENCE. New York: John Wiley and Sons, 1972. xi, 196 p.

This is an analysis of the new town concept, regional and economic planning, employment and population balance, and factor allocation. There is an emphasis on providing an economic analysis.

Feagan, Joe R.; Tilly, Charles; and Williams, Connie. SUBSIDIZING THE POOR: AN EVALUATION OF THE BOSTON HOUSING AUTHORITY PROGRAM. Lexington, Mass.: Lexington Books, 1972. 192 p. Tables and notes. Index.

This is a detailed examination of Boston rent subsidies. It measures the program's impact and success.

Feldt, Allan G. CLUG: COMMUNITY LAND USE GAME, PLAYER'S MANUAL. New York: Free Press, 1972. xi, 260 p.

This is a "classroom tested" urban simulation game designed to be used as a "laboratory experience" for students of urban and regional studies. The game is designed for 5 to 20 players and is recommended for urban economics and sociology as well as urban problems and theory courses.

Fiser, Webb S. MASTERY OF THE METROPOLIS. Englewood Cliffs, N.J.: Prenctice-Hall, 1962. x, 168 p. No index.

Many problems of urban areas are focused on in the eight chapters of this book. Housing, neighborhood, and downtown problems are examined in "Future of the Metropolis," while technical, economic, political, and social characteristics are discussed in "The Context of National Forces." Zoning, education, and land use are dealt with in "The Intermingling of Public and Private." Other chapters explore "The Case of Urban Renewal," "Government Reorganization," and "Citizen Action."

Fusfeld, Daniel R. THE BASIC ECONOMICS OF THE URBAN-RACIAL CRISIS. New York: Dryden Press, 1973. vi, 220 p.

This is a text designed to analyze the riots of 1964-69 and their aftermath. The economic causes are emphasized, and an analytical model of the ghetto economy is developed. Other social and political factors are included in the discussion, but the major elements are economic, developed within the urban framework.

Gans, Herbert. THE LEVITTOWNERS: WAYS OF LIFE AND POLITICS IN A NEW SUBURBAN COMMUNITY. New York: Vintage Books, 1967. xxix, 474 p. References, pp. 452-64. Index, pp. 465-74.

This is an examination of the origin of the community, the quality of life, and the politics and decision making process. The process of change is examined as well.

Gilmore, Harlan W. TRANSPORTATION AND THE GROWTH OF CITIES. Glencoe, Ill.: Free Press, 1953. vi, 170 p. Notes, pp. 147-50. Bibliography, pp. 151-66. Index, pp. 167-70.

The thesis of this monograph is that "community classification, to be realistic, must be done on the basis of a combination of economic and social factors." A scheme is proposed for classifying areas and is followed by a hypothesis on the development of function by community. The first three chapters discuss the history of major transportation innovations and how they apply to the internal structure of the modern metropolis. Chapter 4 accounts for change in communities relative to transportation innovation, while chapter 5 examines the types of towns under these systems. Chapter 6 concludes the work with an examination of the changes taking place within community patterns with respect to transportation innovations.

Hicks, Ursula K. THE LARGE CITY: A WORLD PROBLEM. New York: John Wiley and Sons, 1974. viii, 270 p.

Hicks's focus is on the fiscal dimensions of running a large city, from dealing with problems in the areas of transportation, housing, and transportation to specifics for tax rates.

Hosken, Fran P. THE FUNCTIONS OF CITIES. Cambridge, Mass.: Schenkman Publishing Co., 1973. xi, 276 p.

This is a series of discussions on the function, history, and economy of cities with particular emphasis on problem areas of transportation, education, race relations, health care, and housing. This is written from the perspective of an urban affairs journalist.

Huntoon, Maxwell C., Jr. PUD: A BETTER WAY FOR SUBURBS. Washington, D.C.: Urban Land Institute, 1971. 71 p. Photos. Bibliography, p. 70.

This is a picture book primarily for nonprofessionals examining community development.

League of Women Voters. Education Fund. SUPERCITY/HOMETOWN, U.S.A.: PROSPECTS FOR TWO-TIER GOVERNMENT. New York: Praeger, 1974. xii, 138 p. Paper.

This book deals with the questions of who, within local government, allocates resources and how efficiently do they do it. Metropolitan governments are examined and surveyed, the problems are stated and analyzed, and suggestions for reform are made.

Lipton, Michael. WHY THE POOR STAY POOR: URBAN BIAS IN WORLD DEVELOPMENT. Cambridge, Mass.: Harvard University Press, 1976. 467 p. Notes, pp. 355-424. Tables, pp. 425-50. Index, pp. 451-67.

Discussions of how urban bias works, why it occurred, and how it is maintained are presented in this book. It clearly illustrates how the urban-rural conflict is the most important conflict in poor countries.

Martin, Michael J.C. MANAGEMENT SCIENCE AND URBAN PROBLEMS. Lexington, Mass.: Saxon House, 1974.

This book illustrates the use of mathematical techniques and computer solutions in several urban problem areas. Each project is described, and then the analysis is performed as is a cost-benefit analysis of the proposed solution. There is also a detailed description of the mathematical and computer methods used. Projects include: street lamp replacement, solid waste collection, water resource evaluation, and welfare needs.

Muth, Richard F. CITIES AND HOUSING: THE SPATIAL PATTERN OF URBAN RESIDENTIAL LAND USE. Chicago: University of Chicago Press, 1969. xii, 355 p. Index.

Intercity comparisons of the urban housing pricing system are made using data from 1950 and 1960. Theoretical and empirical elements are treated extensively.

Neubeck, Kenneth J. CORPORATE RESPONSE TO URBAN CRISIS. Lexington, Mass.: Lexington Books, 1974. 160 p. Notes. Appendix. Bibliography. No index.

This is an examination of the ways that "economic institutions" have responded to the urban crisis, using historical material and detailed case studies. Chapters deal with: "Businessmen and Philanthropy: An Historical View" and "The New Corporate Social Responsibility of the 1960's." Case studies are of "The Telephone Company and Inner-City Education," "The Shoe Company and Inner-City Unemployment," and "The Food Company and Inner-City Housing."

Neutze, Grame Max. THE SUBURBAN APARTMENT BOOM: CASE STUDY OF A LAND USE PROBLEM. Baltimore: Resources for the Future, distributed by Johns Hopkins Press, 1968. xii, 184 p. No index.

The objective of this monograph is to shed light on what is occurring in the area of suburban housing, why it is so, and to examine public policy in this area. Nine chapters examine the migration to apartments in the Washington, D.C., Montgomery Co., area. Metropolitan areas are compared, land use decisions are examined, and an optional role for the government in the urban land market is suggested.

Nourse, Hugh O. THE EFFECTS OF PUBLIC POLICY ON HOUSING MARKETS. Lexington, Mass.: Lexington Books, 1973. 140 p. Notes and Tables. Illus. Index.

This work examines contemporary housing policy and analyzes the factors which combine to generate housing problems. Several case studies are used to formulate a regression method to construct a real estate price index, to examine the economics of urban renewal, to suggest the substitution of an income or sales tax for property taxes, and to examine the effects of air pollution on housing and neighborhood change.

Osborn, Frederick J., and Whittick, Arnold. THE NEW TOWNS: THE ANSWER TO MEGALOPOLIS. New York: McGraw-Hill, 1963. xvii, 376 p. Bibliography, pp. 359-62. Index, pp. 363-76.

Each of the 30 chapters of this book looks at new towns in Britain and discusses their impact and significance.

Perloff, Harvey S.; Berg, Tom; Fountain, Robert; Vetter, David; and Weld, John. MODERNIZING THE CENTRAL CITY: NEW TOWNS INTOWN AND BEYOND. Cambridge, Mass.: Ballinger Publishing Co., 1975. xxxi, 414 p. Index, pp. 411-14. Tables, figure, and maps.

This book consists of a review of the New Towns Intown, HUD program for the revitalizing of the central city from its beginning and in light of the lessons from past central city development programs. Part I contains three chapters on NTIT as demonstration projects, reviewing case studies, program implications, and the economics of NTIT. Part II deals with the lessons of urban renewal and model cities programs. Part III presents a programmatic approach to central city development, complete with several case studies. The book concludes with sections on "Special Studies" and a presentation of the authors "Summary and Recommendations." Bibliographies are included at the end of each part.

Peterson, George E.; Solomon, Arthur P.; Madjid, Hadi; and Apgar, William C., Jr. PROPERTY TAXES, HOUSING, AND THE CITIES. Lexington, Mass.: Lexington Books, 1973. 160 p. Notes, tables, figures, and appendixes. No index.

The authors examine the property tax system in urban areas and judge it to be unfair and unfairly administered. Interviews with housing investigators and government officials are integrated with economic theory and policy in this analysis. Ten cities are examined, and each is found to have significant shortcomings in their property tax schemes. Alternatives to the property tax are suggested as is a reform of the property tax system.

Robinson, Albert J. ECONOMIES AND NEW TOWNS: A COMPARATIVE STUDY OF THE UNITED STATES, THE UNITED KINGDOM, AND AUSTRALIA. New York: Praeger, 1975. vi, 142 p. No index.

The goals of new towns or "reverse growth" are examined as an established method of dealing with urban growth. The characteristics, trends, and results of the new town concept are examined of Great Britain, North America, and Australia.

Rossi, Peter H.; Berk, Richard A.; and Eidson, Bettye K. THE ROOTS OF URBAN DISCONTENT, PUBLIC POLICY, MUNICIPAL INSTITUTIONS AND THE GHETTO. New York: John Wiley and Sons, 1974. xxv, 524 p. Index, pp. 449-524.

This book stems from sample data collected in 15 cities with the intent of examining the daily life of the poor and of minorities to see if there are differences in individual cities. Considerations within each of the cities included local government, the economic base, and institutions representing ghetto life.

Rothenberg, Jerome. ECONOMIC EVALUATION OF URBAN RENEWAL: CONCEPTUAL FOUNDATION OF BENEFIT-COST ANALYSIS. Washington, D.C.: Brookings Institution, 1967. xiii, 290 p. Index, pp. 277-90.

This is an examination of the benefit measures arising from the 1949 Urban Renewal programs and the complications which resulted. Alternatives, methods, and a review of the program are discussed, as is the criteria, goals, and benefit measures of the program.

Sackery, Charles. THE POLITICAL ECONOMY OF URBAN POVERTY. New York: W.W. Norton and Company, 1973. xii, 172 p. Selected Bibliography, pp. 145-64. Index, pp. 165-72.

This is a study of the causes, composition, and dimensions of poverty in cities which emphasizes that the methods of study, the explanatory causes and data limitations contribute to the problem. Sackery is critical of liberal reforms and suggests radical solutions to the problem of urban poverty. The five chapters of the book are devoted to "Counting the Urban Poor and Explaining Their Poverty," "Poverty of Urban Black People," "Economics and Black Poverty: The Methodology of Contemporary Liberal Economies,"

"Liberal Remedies for Urban Poverty," and "On Revolutionary Politics: A Short Political Autobiography."

Schnore, Leo F. THE URBAN SCENE, HUMAN ECOLOGY, AND DEMOG-RAPHY. New York: Free Press, 1965. x, 374 p.

This is the result of Schnore's ten-year search for order in the urban system. Topics include demography, human ecology and its myths, suburbanization, urban function and growth, race, and so on. A combination of socioeconomic elements of urban develop-ment are represented.

Schlomo, Angel, and Hyman, Geoffrey M. URBAN TRANSPORT EXPENDITURES. A paper presented to the 11th European Conference of the Regional Science Association, Rome, August, 1971. London: Centre for Environmental Studies, 1971. 34 p. Bibliography, pp. 33-4.

Sobin, Dennis P. THE FUTURE OF AMERICAN SUBURBS: SURVIVAL OR EXTINCTION. Port Washington, N.Y.: National University Publications, 1971. 152 p.

The origins, perceptions, psyche, economics, and alternatives to suburbs are examined in this work. Their growth in population and in employment opportunities are dealt with, as is their relation-ship to the central city.

Stanback, Thomas M., Jr., and Knight, Richard. SUBURBANIZATION AND THE CITY. New York: Allanheld, Osmun Co., and Universe Books, 1976. xviii, 230 p. Index, pp. 227-30.

This study focuses on the role of manpower resources in the pro-cesses of suburban expansion. Data were examined for ten of the nation's largest suburban rings. The framework for the study in-cludes the dynamic relations between suburbanization and the city. Chapters examine: "The Nature of Metropolitan Development," "Transportation, Institutions, and Other Factors Influencing Subur-banization," "Industrial Characteristics," "Occupational Character-istics and Commuter Flows," "Labor Market Characteristics," "Labor Market Flows," "The Unskilled Worker in Cities and Suburbs," and "Metropolis at the Crossroads." Summaries and references are found at the end of most chapters.

Starr, Roger. URBAN CHOICES: THE CITY AND ITS CRITICS. Baltimore: Pelican Books, 1969. 284 p. Index, pp. 279-84. Paper.

Many of the problems of urban areas are dealt with, including housing, unemployment, racial tensions, poverty, transportation, and air and water pollution. Starr argues that the critics of urban life, such as J. Jacobs, H. Gans, and L. Mumford, are much too limited in their approach to the urban predicament in terms of economic and social change. This book was published in hard cover as THE LIVING END.

Sternlieb, George. HOUSING DEVELOPMENT AND MUNICIPAL COSTS. New Brunswick, N.J.: Rutgers University Press, 1973. 500 p. Index.

This is a look at local fiscal problems and the linkage between future housing development on education and other expenditures.

Sternlieb, George; Burchell, Robert W.; and Sagalyn, Lynne B. THE AFFLUENT SUBURB: PRINCETON. New Brunswick, N.J.: Transaction, 1971. 259 p. Index.

This is a statistical survey of Princeton, N.J., designed for dealing with the "future" urban migrations and to allow realistic housing and transportation policies to develop.

Sternlieb, George, and Sagalyn, Lynne B. ZONING AND HOUSING COSTS: THE IMPACT OF LAND USE CONTROLS ON HOUSING PRICE. New Brunswick, N.J.: Rutgers University Press, 1973. 132 p. Index.

While examining the effects of zoning ordinances and housing prices in urban areas, the book also explores the effects the laws have had on low income and minority groups. Questions of economic or ecological necessity are examined as well.

Stone, Clarence N. ECONOMIC GROWTH AND NEIGHBORHOOD DISCONTENT: SYSTEM BIAS IN THE URBAN RENEWAL PROGRAM OF ATLANTA. Chapel Hill: University of North Carolina Press, 1976. xv, 256 p. Appendixes, pp. 217-26. Notes, pp. 227-42. Bibliography, pp. 243-52. Index, pp. 253-56. Tables and maps.

This is a report of research which examines why Atlanta urban development neglected the poor neighborhoods. Community power and politics provide the answer.

Traviss, Irene. TECHNOLOGY AND THE CITY. Cambridge: Harvard University Press, 1970. 53 p.

Tretten, Rudie W. CITIES IN CRISIS: DECAY OR RENEWAL. Englewood Cliffs, N.J.: Prentice-Hall, 1970. 122 p.

This is a group of essays at an elementary or precollege level giving a socioeconomic perspective to the urban crisis.

U.S. National Commission of Urban Problems. REBUILDING THE AMERICAN CITY. Washington, D.C.: U.S. Government Printing Office, 1969. xi, 504 p. Paper.

This is an analysis of the urban scene after the urban riots of the late 60's. Economic, social, and political elements are dealt with.

Vernon, Raymond. THE MYTH AND REALITY OF OUR URBAN PROBLEMS. Cambridge: Harvard University Press, 1962. vii, 91 p. Index, pp. 84-91.

This monograph stems from a series of lectures on the New York Metropolitan Study given by Vernon and focuses on various forces in the urban environment. The growth of the "hinterland," land use planning, mass transportation, and the movement of people are some of the topics covered.

Weaver, Robert C. THE URBAN COMPLEX: HUMAN VALUES IN URBAN LIFE. Garden City, N.Y.: Anchor Books, 1966. xiv, 303 p. Index of Names, pp. 295-96. Index of Subjects, pp. 297-303.

This is a multidisciplinary examination of urban areas which discusses the "Urban Frontier," urban renewal, planning and research, "Economic Considerations," and the future of the urban complex.

Whyte, William H. THE LAST LANDSCAPE. Garden City, N.Y.: Doubleday and Co., 1968. vi, 376 p. Bibliography, pp. 355-63. Index, pp. 364-76.

The 20 chapters of this work examine a variety of land uses within urban areas. It is a lay approach to land use planning of a post-industrial society.

Zehner, Robert B. ACCESS, TRAVEL AND TRANSPORTATION IN NEW COMMUNITIES. New Communities Research Series. Cambridge, Mass.: Ballinger, 1977. xxxii, 217 p. Figures. Subject Reference, pp. 209-12. Index, pp. 213-17.

The focus of this study is an examination of 13 nonfederally funded planned communities and access to them. Chapters examine the "Availability of Neighborhood and Community Facilities," "Employment and the Journey to Work," "Local Transportation," "Auto Ownership and Mileage," and "Transportation for Selected Resident Groups." Appendixes are devoted to "Sampling and Data Collection Procedures," "New Communities and Their Paired Conventional Communities," "Supplementary Tables," and the "Household Survey Questionnaire."

This book is one of a series on New Communities. Others are listed below:

ECONOMIC INTEGRATION IN NEW COMMUNITIES: AN EVALUATION OF FACTORS AFFECTING POLICIES AND IMPLEMENTATION, by Helene V. Smookler. Cambridge, Mass.: Ballinger, 1977.
HEALTH CARE IN NEW COMMUNITIES, by Norman H. Loewenthal and Raymond J. Burley III. Cambridge, Mass.: Ballinger, 1976.
INDICATORS OF THE QUALITY OF LIFE IN NEW COMMUNITIES, by Robert B. Zehner. Cambridge, Mass.: Ballinger, 1976.
NEW COMMUNITIES U.S.A., by R. Burley and W. Weiss. Lexington, Mass.: Lexington Books, 1976.

RECREATION AND LEISURE IN NEW COMMUNITIES, by Raymond J. Burley III. Cambridge, Mass.: Ballinger, 1976.
RESIDENTIAL MOBILITY IN NEW COMMUNITIES: AN ANALYSIS OF RECENT IN-MOVES AND PROSPECTIVE OUT MOVES, by Edward J. Kaiser. Cambridge, Mass.: Ballinger, 1977.
SCHOOLS IN NEW COMMUNITIES, by Raymond J. Burley III and Thomas G. Donnelly. Cambridge, Mass.: Ballinger, 1977.

Chapter 6
URBAN ECONOMICS:
INDUSTRIAL AND SPATIAL PERSPECTIVES

Alexandersson, Grennar. THE INDUSTRIAL STRUCTURE OF AMERICAN CITIES: A GEOGRAPHIC STUDY OF URBAN ECONOMY IN THE UNITED STATES. Stockholm: Almquist and Wiksell, 1956. 134 p. Maps and tables.

The purpose of this report is to analyze the distribution of urban population in an industrialized country. A detailed analysis is made of each industry for cities in the United States with population over 1,000,000.

Bergsman, Joel; Greenston, Peter; and Healey, Robert. EXPLAINING THE ECONOMIC STRUCTURES OF METROPOLITAN AREAS, WORKING PAPER. Washington, D.C.: Urban Institute, 1971. 43 p.

This paper contains the initial steps toward the development of an econometric model asking: "What industries are located in what kind of cities?" There are 69 groups of industries used as dependent variables, with city size, income potential, distance, wage rates, and climate serving as independent variables.

Carter, Harold. THE STUDY OF URBAN GEOGRAPHY. London: Edward Arnold Pub., 1972. xiv, 346 p. Index of Subjects, pp. 337-39. Index of Names, pp. 340-44. Index of Places, pp. 345-46.

Although written for geographers, the subject headings are fare for a number of regional and urban economists. They include: the process of urbanization, urban functions and classification of towns, central place theory, ranking of towns, problems of central place theory, urban land use, the central business district, and so on.

Cutler, Irving. THE CHICAGO-MILWAUKEE CORRIDOR: A GEOGRAPHIC STUDY OF INTERMETROPOLITAN COALESCENSE. Northwestern University Studies in Geography, no. 9. Evanston, Ill.: Northwestern University Press, 1965. 310 p.

Dickinson, Robert E. CITY, REGION AND REGIONALISM: A GEOGRAPHIC CONTRIBUTION TO HUMAN ECOLOGY. New York: Oxford University Press, 1947. xv, 342 p. Index, pp. 327-42.

This is a geographic view of the urban area as a regional center for services, industry, and others. Examples are given illustrating the structure of cities, patterns of location, and the anatomy of a city.

_____. CITY AND REGION; A GEOGRAPHICAL INTERPRETATION. London: Routledge and Kegan Paul, 1964. xx, 588 p. Index, p. 577.

This is a part of the series (CITY AND REGION AND REGIONAL-ISM, 1947) that is concerned with the geographical structure of society based on the premise that a society must be examined in its spatial context prior to the treatment of its problems. Central places are examined in the United States and in West Europe and the spatial context of the book should be of interest to economists.

Goldberg, Michael. INTRAMETROPOLITAN INDUSTRIAL LOCATION: PLANT SIZE AND THE THEORY OF PRODUCTION. Berkley: Center for Real Estate and Urban Economics, Institute of Urban and Regional Development, University of California, 1969. xvi, 242 p. Bibliography, pp. 233-42.

The "Bay Area Simulation" is discussed in this work, with an examination of this large scale land use model. There are sections dealing with location theory, production and cost, intrametropolitan industrial location, the size distribution of plants in a spatial framework, and the data involved in the project. The conclusion aims at a "more general theory of intrametropolitan industrial location."

Hammer, Andrew Marshall. INDUSTRIAL EXODUS FROM CENTRAL CITY: PUBLIC POLICY AND COMPARATIVE COSTS OF LOCATION. Lexington, Mass.: Lexington Books, 1973. xiii, 107 p. Bibliography, pp. 103-7. No index.

This study develops a framework for analyzing the relevant costs of manufacture location. A case study in Boston is used in an attempt to understand what specific inputs affect the variation of costs of production over space. The six chapters examine "Industrial Location Behavior in an Urban Context," "A Tentative Framework for Intrametropolitan Location," "Existing Intra-Urban Cost Differentials: Land, Government Services, Labor," "Multilevel Verses Single Story Construction: The Possibility of a Land-Capital Trade-Off," "Rental Equivalent Costs in Central City and Suburban Locations," and a "Postscript on Central City Subsidy Scheme."

Harris, Curtis C., Jr. THE URBAN ECONOMICS 1985: A MULTIREGIONAL, MULTI-INDUSTRY FORECASTING MODEL. Lexington, Mass.: Lexington Books, 1973. xvi, 230 p. Index, pp. 227-30. Figures and Tables.

This is the second book by the same author which continues with the theme of locational analysis and adds additional economic data. Only SMSA's are examined, and the model developed assumes that changes in industry location are the predominant forces in the growth or decline of a region. The model is developed, as is the theoretical framework and data estimates. Finally, forecasts are made using the model. The author suggests that a major use of this model will be in regional impact analysis.

Harvey, David. SOCIETY: THE CITY AND THE SPACE-ECONOMY OF URBANISM. Washington, D.C.: Association of American Geographers, 1972. 56 p. Bibliography, pp. 55-56. Illus.

Johnson, James H. URBAN GEOGRAPHY: AN INTRODUCTORY ANALYSIS. New York: Pergamon Press, 1968. xv, 188 p. Notes on Further Reading, pp. 183-84. Index, pp. 185-88.

This work draws on many others in its attempt to "produce some order out of a diverse field." "Factors in Urban Growth" presents some information about early urban development as well as discussing current factors relevant to the growth issue. "Urban Society and Urban Form" discusses planning and transportation issues from the colonial cities. Next are chapters on the demographic and occupational characteristics of urban areas. "Location, Spacing and Size of Urban Settlements" discusses central place theory, urban hierarchies and zones of influence. Various areas of the city are examined in the next three chapters, particularly the central city, suburbs, and manufacturing areas. Johnson concludes by discussing "Theories of Urban Structure."

Kain, John F. ESSAYS ON URBAN SPATIAL STRUCTURE. Cambridge, Mass.: Ballinger Publishing Co., 1975. xx, 412 p. Notes, pp. 363-406. Index, pp. 407-410. Figures and Tables.

This collection of seventeen essays was written over the last ten years. Major headings include: "The Location of Jobs" (two essays), "Effects of Racial Discrimination" (four essays), "An Analysis of Urban Housing Markets" (five essays), and "Urban Transportation" (three essays). Several of the essays are coauthored, many are reprints, while others are revisions of earlier work. The perspective of these essays is one which illuminate the growth of the early 1960s and the crisis and shift of priorities of the late 1960s and 1970s.

Kozlowski, Jurek, and Hughes, James T. THRESHOLD ANALYSIS. London: Architectural Press, 1972. 286 p. Notes, pp. 269-79. Bibliography, pp. 280-83. Index, pp. 284-86.

The aim of this book is "to provide a more comprehensive and sophisticated elaboration of threshold theory and analysis," and to present simple rules for its application in urban and regional planning. The 13 chapters are focused on three main areas: "The

Theoretical Background"; "Evaluation," with applications to Poland, Scotland, Yugoslavia, and Ireland; and "Development."

McCrystal, Lawrence P. CITY, TOWN OR COUNTRY: THE ECONOMICS OF CONCENTRATION AND DISPERSAL, WITH PARTICULAR REFERENCE TO SOUTH AFRICA. Capetown: A.A. Balkema, 1969. 279 p. Bibliography, pp. 264-76. Index, pp. 277-79.

The purpose of this study is to establish the factors and forces which underlie the location decision of businessmen and to clarify the process of regional economic growth in South Africa. The four main parts examine the "Economic Growth Patterns," "Economics of Urbanization," "Economics of Location," and the "Dispersal of Economic Activity."

Mundell, Lewis. INDUSTRIAL LOCATION DECISIONS/DETROIT COMPARED WITH ATLANTA AND CHICAGO. New York: Praeger, 1975. x, 121 p.

These are the results of a 1972 study of the three urban areas with a manufacturing sample from Detroit compared to Atlanta and Chicago. Topics included in this book are the potential shift of industrial employment from Detroit, various factors present in plant location decision, the advantages and disadvantages of Detroit, and the quality of life. The book presents a contrast of the manufacturing and industrial bases as to locations, scale economies, quality of life, and the effects of cyclical and secular fluctuations in economic activity.

Pred, Alan R. THE SPATIAL DYNAMICS OF U.S. URBAN INDUSTRIAL GROWTH 1800-1914: INTERPRETIVE AND THEORETICAL ESSAYS. Cambridge: M.I.T. Press, 1966. x, 255 p. Index, pp. 217-55.

This is a volume of work examining the urban heritage of the United States with an emphasis on process. Three integrated themes, dealing with the spatial dynamics of U.S. urban-industrial growth are utilized. The first deals with the bond between growth and larger concentrations between the Civil War and WWI. The second theme is that of innovation and growth, and the third examines economic and spatial relations.

Smith, David Marshall. INDUSTRIAL LOCATION: AN ECONOMIC GEOGRAPHICAL ANALYSIS. New York: John Wiley and Sons, 1971. xii, 553 p. Bibliography, pp. 519-42. Index, pp. 543-53.

Divided into six parts and containing twenty-seven chapters, the major areas of concentration of this book are: variables in industrial location, the theory of industrial location--approaches and a synthesis, empirical applications (including a number of case studies), alternative approaches (including correlation, regression, L.P. and I-O. analysis), and industrial location economic development and public policy. This is as much for economists as for geographers.

Spiegelman, Robert G. A STUDY OF INDUSTRY LOCATION USING MULTI-PLE REGRESSION TECHNIQUES. Agricultural Economic Report, no. 140. Washington, D.C.: Economic Research Service, U.S.D.A., 1968. 66 p.

> This monograph contains a discussion of the use of multiple regression to analyze change in industrial location and generates a model for estimating changes in industrial location. Also included are ways to use the results of this model.

Steiss, Alan Walter. MODELS FOR ANALYSIS AND PLANNING OF URBAN SYSTEMS. Lexington, Mass.: Lexington Books, 1974. vii, 352 p. Author Index, pp. 347-48. Subject Index, pp. 349-52.

> The concern of this book is the question of urban growth and how it should be handled. The analysis centers around new towns and discusses their roles and effects in the United Kingdom, North America, and Australia.

Stevens, Benjamin H., and Brackett, Carolyn A. INDUSTRIAL LOCATION: A REVIEW AND ANNOTATED BIBLIOGRAPHY OF THEORETICAL, EMPIRICAL AND CASE STUDIES. Philadelphia: Regional Science Research Institute, 1967. 199 p. Subject Index, pp. 191-99.

> This work includes some 850 entries for the scholar interested in location theory. There are listings for those interested in applied research in industrial location and regional economic development.

Stone, P.A. THE STRUCTURE, SIZE AND COSTS OF URBAN SETTLEMENTS. Cambridge, Mass.: Cambridge University Press, 1973. xviii, 302 p. Index, pp. 284-302.

> In this volume, size and form are related to construction costs to examine settlement and planning, the returns, and cost of development.

Struyk, Raymond J., and James, Franklin J. INTRAMETROPOLITAN INDUS-TRIAL LOCATION: THE PATTERN AND PROCESS OF CHANGE. Lexington, Mass.: Lexington Books, 1975. xvi, 191 p. Appendixes, pp. 151-88. Index, pp. 189-91.

> The goal of this work is the "documentation of job location patterns within urban areas, the description and analysis of overall change in these patterns, and the behavior of individual manufacturing establishments that produce these changes." Part I examines the "Trends and Composition of the Spatial Distribution of Manufacturing Employment in Four Metropolitan Areas." These are Cleveland, Minneapolis-St. Paul, Boston, and Phoenix. In part II, the regularities found in part I are examined and hypotheses are generated.

Taylor, T. Griffith. URBAN GEOGRAPHY: A STUDY OF SITE EVOLUTION, PATTERN, AND CLASSIFICATION IN VILLAGES, TOWNS, AND CITIES.

London: Methuen and Co., 1949.   xv, 439 p.   Bibliography, pp. 425-38.
Index, pp. 435-39.

The 20 chapters of this book examine the general features of a
number of cities, their historical growth pattern, cultural traits,
and their topography.

Chapter 7
COLLECTIONS OF ARTICLES, PAPERS, AND ESSAYS

Adams, John S., ed. URBAN POLICYMAKING AND METROPOLITAN DY-
NAMICS: A COMPARATIVE GEOGRAPHICAL ANALYSIS. Cambridge, Mass.:
Ballinger Publishing Co., 1976. xxii, 577 p. Index, pp. 567-77. Figures
and Tables.

> This book is compiled from a geographical perspective. It is a
> part of the comparative metropolitan analysis project sponsored by
> the Association of American Geographers examining the 20 largest
> cities in the United States. The study was designed to assess the
> success of each of the cities in meeting human needs in a spatial
> context. The essays analyze the progress made in urban policy
> during the 1960s in these cities.

Andrews, Richard B., ed. URBAN LAND USE POLICY: THE CENTRAL CITY.
New York: Free Press, 1972. xiii, 285 p. Selected References, p. 276.
Index, pp. 277-85.

> There are 34 readings included in this collection which examines
> central city land use policy. Fifteen essays explore zoning regu-
> lations and policies, ten examine building and housing codes, and
> eight essays deal with taxation.

Arrow, Kenneth J.; March, James G.; Coleman, Jane S.; and Downs, Anthony.
THE URBAN PROCESS AS VIEWED BY THE SOCIAL SCIENCES. Washington,
D.C.: Urban Institute, 1973. 79 p.

> The introduction to these short essays points to the need for "a
> new understanding of the institutions and processes" in the urban
> sphere. The focus here is on the institutions which distribute
> wealth and power and not on wealth and power. Political and
> social factors of the market, as well as the economic, are dis-
> cussed.

Beaton, W. Patrick, ed. MUNICIPAL NEEDS, SERVICES AND FINANCING:
READINGS ON MUNICIPAL EXPENDITURE. New Brunswick, N.J.: Center
for Urban Policy Research, Rutgers University, 1974. 349 p.

The structure of the local public sector is examined in the way that it relates to local problems. Included are discussions of inflation, productivity, unionization, and how local governments must respond to these in the future.

Bergsman, Joel, and Weiner, Howard, eds. URBAN PROBLEMS AND PUBLIC CHOICES. New York: Praeger, 1975. xv, 346 p. Tables and figures.

These seventeen essays run the gamut of subject matter from theoretical models to program design and political bargaining, and they are from the proceedings from a conference on "Urban Growth and Development" held in April, 1973. There are six major parts to the book. They are: I. "Urban Research and Policy Making," II. "Delivery of Public Services," III. "Social and Political Urban Process Models," IV. "The Impact of Public Policies on Urban Markets," V. "Urban Land Use and Transportation," and VI. "Environmental Goals and Urban Development."

Bernstein, Samuel J., and Mellon, W. Giles, eds. SELECTIVE READINGS IN URBAN ANALYSIS. New York: Pergamon, 1977. 380 p. Index.

Urban problems are approached through quantitative methods in this group of readings. The most recent models are included as well as policy studies in health service systems.

Berry, Brian J.L., ed. URBANIZATION AND COUNTERURBANIZATION. Beverly Hills, Calif.: Sage Publications, 1976. 334 p. No Index.

A comparative approach is taken in these essays which examine urban change in the 1970s in affluent economic systems. The first half of the volume contrasts approaches of the East and the West in the first and second worlds, while decolonization and ideological contrasts are the themes emerging from the examination of the third and fourth worlds. Countries which are examined are: the United States, Britain, Brazil, South Africa, Australia, North Africa, West Africa, and China.

Berry, Brian J.L., and Meltzer, Jack, eds. GOALS FOR URBAN AMERICA. Englewood Cliffs, N.J.: Prentice-Hall, 1967. 152 p. No index.

The theme running through this series of essays is that of trouble in urban society, that the "organic socio-economic city is out of phase with political organizations." Since the dynamic process of growth implies social and economic change, new ideas and thinking must emerge to cope with this change. The following essays are included: "The City: Work of Art and Technology," by A. Heckscher; "Urbanization in the Developing World," by D. Owen; "The New Urbanism," by S. Clark; "The States and the Cities--The Unfinished Agenda," by T. Sanford; "National Urban Policy, Appropriate to the American Pattern," by M. Myerson; "Race in the City," by N. Glazer; "Desegregation: What Impact on the Urban Scene," by W. Young; "Policies to Combat Negro Poverty," by R. Kennedy; and "Social and Physical Planning for the Urban Slum" by J. Meltzer and J. Whitley.

Berry, Brian J.L., and Smith, Katherine B., eds. CITY CLASSIFICATION HANDBOOK: METHODS AND APPLICATIONS. New York: Wiley-Interscience, 1972. 394 p.

This series of essays was compiled with the aim of improving the use and utilization of statistical data and methodology, particularly in a computer-oriented environment. The various sections of the book examine the strengths and weaknesses of the methodology in classifying cities, the social and political research potential, and alternative classification criteria.

Blumstein, James F., and Martin, Eddie J., eds. THE URBAN SCENE IN THE SEVENTIES. Nashville, Tenn.: Vanderbilt University Press, 1974. xi, 256 p.

This series of essays deals primarily with economic policy toward poverty. Existing programs are evaluated, along with other strategies and alternatives. These essays stem from a Conference on Public Policy for Urban Minorities and Poor held at Fisk University in 1972.

Boulding, Kenneth E.; Pfaff, Martin; and Pfaff, Anita, eds. TRANSFERS IN AN URBANIZED ECONOMY: THEORIES AND EFFECTS OF THE GRANTS ECONOMY. Belmont, Calif.: Wadsworth Publishing Co., 1973. iv, 376 p. No index.

This group of papers is devoted to examining nonmarket redistribution which occurs in the United States particularly as they are characterized by elements of a urbanized economy. The readings are grouped into five parts: "Exploitative Transfers in Metropoles," (2 essays), "Voluntary and Involuntary Transfers through Charity and the Tax System: Their Effects on Urban Poverty," (4 essays), "Tax Transfers and Educational Policy," (5 essays), and "Transfers as Instruments of Urban Ecological Policy" (5 essays).

Bourne, Larry P., ed. INTERNAL STRUCTURE OF THE CITY: READINGS ON SPACE AND ENVIRONMENT. New York: Oxford University Press, 1971. vii, 528 p.

This is a series of readings dealing with the urban process. Location theory, land use, and population are examined in the first section. This is followed by discussions of interaction within the city. Concluding essays examine the future and role of the urban area. These are essays by R. Vernon, B.J.L. Berry, W. Alonso, S. Chapin, C. Tiebout and others.

Bourne, Larry P.; MacKinnon, Ross D.; Siegel, Jay; and Simmons, James W., eds. URBAN FUTURES FOR CENTRAL CANADA: PERSPECTIVES ON FORE-CASTING URBAN GROWTH AND FORM. Toronto: University of Toronto Press, 1974. viii, 367 p.

> The objective of this series of essays is to examine the future of urban areas in a rapidly growing and changing environment to better understand the present and recent past. Three themes run through the essays, forecasting, consequences of trends, and the role of public policy. The first part, devoted to "Forecasts of Urban Growth," contains four essays which define the future of the urban system, forecast the urban population, and make a long-run employment forecast for the Toronto area. Part 2 deals with "Growth and the Urban System" and looks at the urban hierarchy, the components of intraurban migration, intracity linkages, and the effects of public policy in the future urban system. The third part examines growth and urban form and contains four essays.

Brown, Alan A.; Licari, Joseph A.; and Neuberger, Egon, eds. URBAN AND SOCIAL ECONOMICS IN MARKET AND PLANNED ECONOMIES. Vol. 1: POLICY, PLANNING, AND DEVELOPMENT. New York: Praeger, 1974. xxvi, 445 p. Name Index, pp. 433-38. Subject Index, pp. 439-45. Tables and figures.

> This is the first of two volumes generated from the Windsor Conference on Comparative Urban Economics and Development. These essays attempt to put methodological and empirical urban studies into a comparative context, using case studies illustrating urban concerns and policy from several countries. Topic headings are: urban economics and policy, urban planning, urbanization and development and a comparative analysis of urbanized areas. H. Perloff, B. Chinitz, F. and I. Adelman, E. Mills, J. Kain, and B. Harris are among the contributors.

_____. URBAN AND SOCIAL ECONOMICS IN MARKET AND PLANNED ECONOMIES. Vol. 2: HOUSING, INCOME, AND ENVIRONMENT. New York: Praeger, 1972. xxv, 340 p. Name Index, pp. 333-36. Subject Index, pp. 337-40.

> These 15 essays deal with housing and urban renewal, the sources and nature of income distribution, poverty and the aged, work incentives, and long-term perspectives on growth. Contributors include: J. Rothenberg, J. Tinberger, and W. Vickrey.

Bryce, Herrington J., ed. SMALL CITIES IN TRANSITION: THE DYNAMICS OF GROWTH AND DECLINE. Cambridge: Ballinger Publishing Co., 1977. xxiv, 418 p. Notes, pp. 381-96. Index, pp. 397-412.

> This collection of articles was prepared for a symposium examining the growth of small cities. They examine the future of this trend, the role of federal and state governments, fiscal and planning

problems and other factors relevant to small cities. Contributors include: W. Alonso, H. Bryce, N. Beckman, W. Thompson, S. Sacks, W. Hirsch, B. Berry, B. Chinitz. There are 16 chapters included in the seven parts. Major parts include: "Population Growth, Decline and Policies," "Migration and Population Policies," "Economic Growth and Decline," "Economic Characteristics of Small Cities," "Federal Impact on Cities," "The Metropolitan Setting and the Future of Small Cities," and "Conclusions: Planning for the Future."

Burgess, Ernest W., ed. THE URBAN COMMUNITY. Chicago: University of Chicago Press, 1925. xii, 268 p. Author Index, pp. 265-66. Subject Index, pp. 267-78.

This is a group of selected papers from the American Sociological Association meetings in 1925. The focus is on human economy and the "Urban Community's Spatial Path and Moral Order." The 30 essays have a general social science bias.

Burnly, I.H., ed. URBANIZATION IN AUSTRALIA: THE POST WAR EXPERIENCE. Cambridge: Cambridge University Press, 1974. 248 p.

Cameron, Gordon C., and Wingo, Lowdon, Jr., eds. CITIES, REGIONS AND PUBLIC POLICY. Edinburgh: Oliver and Boyd, 1973. xxii, 337 p. Index, pp. 333-37.

These papers were generated at a conference in Glasgow of 50 leading U.K., U.S., and European scholars discussing the theme "Economic Research and National Urban Development Strategies." There are 15 major papers falling under the broad headings (1) positive and normative questions at a rational level, (2) relationships between individual regions and urban development, and (3) regional problems and policies the context of the U.K. The second part of the book contains a summary of the conference proceedings. Authors include: L. Wingo, R. Richardson, W. Thompson, J. Bergsman, and G. Cameron.

Canty, Donald, ed. THE NEW CITY. New York: Praeger for Urban America, 1969. 180 p. Index, pp. 177-80.

These essays deal with the "Process of Urbanization," the "Concept of Urbanization," "Social Strategy and Urban Growth," "New Cities and National Strategies," "Some Origins of Growth," and "Findings and Recommendations." An underlying theme that is found running through these papers is that urbanization patterns need to change to avoid further waste of resources and energy.

Chapin, F. Stuart, Jr., and Weiss, Shirley F., eds. URBAN GROWTH DYNAMICS IN A REGIONAL CLUSTER OF CITIES. New York: John Wiley and Sons, 1962. x, 484 p.

This collection of essays is a general social sciences examination of the urban process, including behavior patterns, urban development, and value systems. The essays are based on studies of the Piedmont Crescent area of the Carolinas.

Chard, Jim, and York, Jon, eds. CRISIS AND OPPORTUNITY. Belmont, Calif.: Dickenson Publishing Co., 1969. xix, 251 p. No index.

Chartrand, Robert Lee, ed. HOPE FOR CITIES: A SYSTEMS APPROACH TO HUMAN NEEDS. New York: Spartan Books, 1971. xxv, 731 p. Index, pp. 706-31.

The report of the Washington Operations Research Council dealing with the economic and political aspects of pollution, crime, housing, planning, and others in the urban area.

Chinitz, Benjamin, ed. CITY AND SUBURBS: THE ECONOMICS OF METRO-POLITAN GROWTH. Englewood Cliffs, N.J.: Prentice-Hall, 1964. viii, 181 p.

A collection of essays by urban specialists such as E. Hoover, R. Vernon, Meyer and Wood on urban structure, growth, transportation, planning.

Clawson, Marion, ed. MODERNIZING URBAN LAND POLICY. Baltimore: John Hopkins Press for Resources for the future, 1973. vii, 248 p. Index, pp. 241-48.

These papers are the result of a forum held by RFF to review the problems of urban land policy, "particularly the exclusionary aspects of land zoning and associated local land controls." The collection of papers includes: "Public Land, Urban Development Policy and the American Planning Tradition" by J. Reps; "Housing and Associated Problems of Minorities" by R. Weaver, "Economic and Social Costs of Residential Segregation" by W. Steger, "Tax Reform to Release Land" by M. Gaffney, "Legal Assaults on Municipal Land Use Regulation" by I. Heyman, "Casting the Courts in a Land Use Reform Effort: A Starring Role or a Supporting Part?" by K. Fessler, "Ecology and Housing: Virtues in Conflict" by R. Babcock and K. Callies, and "Alternatives for Future Urban Land Policy" by M. Clawson and H. Perloff.

David, Kingsley, ed. CITIES: THEIR ORIGIN, GROWTH AND HUMAN IMPACT. San Francisco: W. H. Freeman and Co., 1973. 297 p. Bibliographies, pp. 289-94. Index, pp. 295-97.

This volume contains a selection of articles which have appeared in SCIENTIFIC AMERICAN which are related to cities. These 27 articles are grouped into five major headings: "The Earliest Cities,"

"Population, Health and the City Environment," "Urban Transport and City Planning," "Cities in the Developing World," and "Group Relations in Cities."

Edel, Mathew, and Rothenberg, Jerome, eds. READINGS IN URBAN ECO-NOMICS. New York: Macmillan Co., 1972. vi, 602 p. No index.

Many of the forty readings contained in this book are reprints of articles, several of which are "classics," in the area of urban economics. This collection provides a wide variety of perspectives and analysis of urban problems. This reader is designed to supplement courses in urban economics. A few readings use mathematical models and are suitable for graduate and advanced students. Topic areas include: "Location Theory and Metropolitan Growth," "Intra-urban Location and Land Use," "Housing," Segregation and Ghetto Poverty," "Congestion and Pollution," "Urban Transportation," and "Urban Public Finance." Contributors to the volume include: W. Alonso, R. Vernon, T. Koopmans and M. Beckman, T. Moses, C. Tiebout, B. Chinitz, E. Mills, M. Edel, R. Muth, W. Hirsch, W. Vickery, and J. Heilbrun.

Elderedge, H. Wentworth, ed. TAMING MEGALOPOLIS. Vol. 1: WHAT IS AND WHAT COULD BE. New York: Frederick A. Praeger, 1967. xv, 585 p. Index, pp. 577-85.

This first of two volumes contains essays on the political, economic, and planning aspects of urban areas. The three are integrated into the essays and provide a "unified many pronged attack." Regional and national aspects are examined in the context of urban problems as well.

_____. TAMING MEGALOPOLIS. Vol. 2: HOW TO MANAGE AN URBAN-IZED WORLD. New York: Frederick A. Praeger, 1967. xv, 581 p. Index, pp. 574-581.

This is a continuation of volume I with essays by J. Gottman, E. Banfield, H. Perloff, F. S. Chapin, B. Harris and W. Alonso. The economic, political, and planning themes continue to run through this volume and relate it to volume I.

Elias, C. E., Jr.; Gillies, James; and Riemer, Svend, eds. METROPOLIS: VALUES IN CONFLICT. Belmont, Calif.: Wadsworth Publishing Co., 1964. x, 362 p.

This collection of essays deals with the problems and conflicts which arise from increased urbanization. The introduction gives a historical perspective to the problem, and the remainder is devoted to an elaboration of the issues and the dialogue which surrounds urban problem. Urban design, the automobile, housing, urban government, and politics are among the issues raised. There is little economic analysis.

Fickers, Victor B., and Graves, Herbert S., eds. SOCIAL SCIENCE AND URBAN CRISES: INTRODUCTORY READINGS. New York: Macmillan Co., 1971. xviii, 461 p. Suggested Readings, pp. 457-61.

This book was designed for college freshmen who will encounter little else in the realm of the social sciences. Sections are included on the city in history, the city today, urban ethnic groups, government, poverty and welfare, education and unemployment, the urban tax jungle, the ghetto, urban problems, and the city of tomorrow.

Frieden, Bernard J., and Morris, Robert, eds. URBAN PLANNING AND SOCIAL POLICY. New York: Basic Books, 1968. xvii, 476 p. Index, pp. 459.

Problems inherent in cities are examined by noted social scientists who are actively involved in various areas of urban studies. The 28 essays include proposals for dealing with housing, race, poverty, and offer suggestions for establishing guidelines for social policy.

Frieden, Bernard J., and Nash, William W., Jr., eds. SHAPING AN URBAN FUTURE: ESSAYS IN MEMORY OF CATHERINE BAUER WUSTER. Cambridge: M.I.T. Press, 1969.

These readings stem from a lecture series at M.I.T. designed to explore possible urban futures and choices. Specific areas of focus are: housing, problems of minorities, urban growth, urban development and its management, and alternative futures for urban areas. Contributors include L. Wingo, N. Beckman, and B. Harris.

Gappert, Garry, and Rose, Harold M., eds. THE SOCIAL ECONOMY OF CITIES. Urban Affairs Annual Reviews. Beverly Hills, Calif.: Sage Publications, 1975. 640 p.

These essays examine theoretical rather than empirical aspects of the urban area. Social and economic relationships are considered within spatial bounds. Topic areas include poverty, urban spatial change, housing markets, and several dimensions of the urban populations. Contributors include B.J.L. Berry and H. Nourse.

Garrison, W. L., and Marble, D. F., eds. QUANTITATIVE GEOGRAPHY. Part I: ELEVEN ESSAYS ON ECONOMIC AND CULTURAL TOPICS. Northwestern University Studies in Geography, no. 13. Evanston, Ill.: Northwestern University, Geography Department, 1967. 288 p.

Authors include Hagerstrand, Marble, Nystuen, Morrill, Beckmann, Mayfield, Thomas, Warntz, and B.J.L. Berry.

Gibbs, Jack P., ed. URBAN RESEARCH METHODS. Princeton, N.J.: D. Van Nostrand Co., 1961. xxii, 647 p. Bibliography, pp. 581-622. Index, pp. 623-47.

These readings look at demographic, ecological, and economic aspects of the urban area and the process of urbanization. Examinations of techniques and processes and procedures from professional journals are included as well as essays written specifically for this volume. The seven major divisions include discussions on urban units, their characteristics, their spatial structure, and urban and rural contrasts. W. Isard, J. Mattila, W. Thompson, K. Davis, O.D. Duncanaand, and D. Bogue are contributors.

Gordon, David M., ed. PROBLEMS IN POLITICAL ECONOMY: AN URBAN PERSPECTIVE. 2d ed. Lexington, Mass.: D.C. Heath, 1977. xvi, 528 p. Paper. No index.

Each of the eight major sections contains a lengthy introduction by the editor and a bibliography. Each of the sections analyzes the problem area on each of four levels. First, there is an application of the general analytical perspective. Next, each problem is defined, and its magnitudes are examined by using current data. The third level contains the core of the analytical discussion, and the fourth examines various "visions" for solutions to the problem. Specific areas of focus are: "General Perspectives, Radical, Liberal, and Conservative," "Employment," "Race," "Education," "Poverty and Welfare," "Crime," "Health," and "Housing." Radical, liberal, and conservative approaches are contained throughout with selections by: M. Friedman, E. Banfield, W. Heller, A. Okun, P. Sweezy, R. Leftwich, M. Feldstein, B. Bluestone, M. Piore, and others.

Gorham, William, and Glazer, Nathan, eds. THE URBAN PREDICAMENT. Washington, D.C.: Urban Institute, 1976. xvii, 363 p. Index, pp. 357-63.

This is a "comprehensive social report on the present quality of life in America." The selection of topics includes finance, housing, crime, education, and transportation. Contributors include: G. Peterson, F. deLeeuw, A. Schnore, J. Wilson and B. Bolard, J. Coleman and S. Kelly, M. Kemp, and M. Chisholm.

Greenberg, Michael B., ed. READINGS IN URBAN ECONOMICS AND SPATIAL PATTERNS. New Brunswick, N.J.: Center for Urban Policy Research, Rutgers University, 1974. 328 p. Supplementary Bibliography, pp. 319-28.

This readings text is designed for those interested in a variety of urban fields, such as urban planning, urban studies, urban economics, and urban geography. Elementary economic theory, methodology, and a systems approach to issues of industrial location, externalities, growth dynamics, and land use provide a framework for the essays. Authors whose work is included are: E. Hoover, W. Alonso, B.J.L. Berry, and N. Hansen.

Grieson, Ronald E., ed. PUBLIC AND URBAN ECONOMICS: ESSAYS IN HONOR OF WILLIAM S. VICKREY. Lexington, Mass.: Lexington Books, 1976. ix, 421 p.

Divided into two parts, public economics and urban economics, these nine essays deal specifically with issues in urban economics. Topics include: crime prevention and police service production, ethnicity and residential location, externalities, taxation policies and effects, and spatial equilibrium. These are works by: J. Kain, R. Grieson, W. Hirsch, E.J. Mishan, R. Muth, and J. Rothenberg.

_____. URBAN ECONOMICS: READINGS AND ANALYSIS. Boston: Little Brown and Co., 1973. x, 453 p, Paper.

Grieson has produced a combination text-readings book whose eleven chapters contain lengthy introductions and thirty essays designed for use in urban economics courses. The verbal "theoretical rigor" is acceptable for more advanced courses. Chapter headings are: "Allocation of Resources in Central Cities," "Growth Income and Economic Stability," "Location and Land Use," "Transportation," "Zoning, Housing Markets and Urban Renewal," "Pollution," "Discrimination," "Metropolitanism," "Urban Public Finance," and a "Methodological Appendix: Marginal Analysis, Benefit-Cost, and the Social Rate of Discount." Selections are included by: W. Thompson, C. Tiebout, B. Chinitz, E. Mills, W. Alonso, J. Meyer and J. Kain, W. Vickery, R. Muth, E. Mishan, R. Lampman, L. Thurow, J. Margolis, D. Netzer, and others.

Hadden Jeffrey K.; Masotti, Louis H; and Larson, Calvin J., eds. METROPOLIS IN CRISIS: SOCIAL AND POLITICAL PERSPECTIVES. Itasca, Ill.: F.E. Peacock Publishers, 1971. xxii, 622 p. Bibliography, pp. 580-608. Name Index, pp. 609-14. Subject Index, pp. 615-22.

Though most of the 67 readings in this collection offer a more social science approach to urban problems, a few are of interest to economists desiring to supplement an introductory urban economics course.

Harloe, Michael, ed. CAPTIVE CITIES: STUDIES IN THE POLITICAL ECONOMY OF CITIES AND REGIONS. New York: John Wiley and Sons, 1977. 218 p. Bibliographic references, pp. 210-12. Index, pp. 213-18

This volume contains ten essays and includes discussions of the new trends in urban sociology, drawing on the Weberian and Marxist approaches. Sponsored by the International Sociological Association Research Committee on Sociology of Regional and Urban Development, the essays relate urban development to society as a whole and look at the relationship of urban and regional problems to urban growth.

Harring, Joseph E., ed. URBAN AND REGIONAL ECONOMICS: PERSPEC-
TIVES FOR PUBLIC ACTION. Boston: Houghton Mifflin, 1972. viii, 307 p.
Bibliography, pp. 303-07. No index.

Experts in urban economics have used macro and micro techniques
to seek solutions to a variety of problem areas. The 32 readings
are couched in four main sections. Part I gives an overview of
the urban area and contains essays by R. Vernon and J. Jacobs.
Part II is devoted to urban issues of poverty, unemployment, housing, education, and crime, and essays by M. Friedman, J.
Spengler, S. Sternlieb, J. Meyer, and J. Kain are included.
Urban financing is the topic of Part III, with contributions by
J. Heilbrun, D. Netzer, W. Heller, and W. Vickrey. Part IV
examines the regional context with essays by C. Tiebout, D.
North, and the CED.

Hauser, Philip M., and Schnore, Leo F., eds. THE STUDY OF URBANIZATION.
New York: John Wiley and Sons, 1965. viii, 554 p. No index.

The 14 papers in this volume are the product of the Social Science
Research Council and explore "The Study of Urbanization in the
Social Sciences," "Comparative Urban Research," and "Selected
Research Problems." Contributors include: C. Glaab, R. Vernon
and E. Hoover, L. Schnore, B. Berry, W. Thompson, P. Hauser,
and E. Lampard.

Herbert, D.T., and Johnston, R.J., eds. SOCIAL AREAS IN CITIES. Vol. 1:
SPATIAL PROCESSES AND FORM. New York: John Wiley and Sons, 1976.
xiii, 281 p. Index, pp. 273-81.

This series allows for a more in-depth presentation of topics of
interest to many urban scholars. This volume includes work rele-
vant to sociologists, economists, psychologists, and political econ-
omists. The essays include: "Sociospatial Differentation and the
Use of Services" by C.J. Thomas, "Political Behavior and the
Presidential Mosaic" by R.J. Johnson, "Social Deviance in the
City" by D.T. Herbert, and "Urban Education" by D.T. Herbert.
There are extensive references at the end of each selection.

_____. SOCIAL AREAS IN CITIES. Vol. 2: SPATIAL PERSPECTIVES ON
PROBLEMS AND POLICIES. New York: John Wiley and Sons, 1976. viii,
243 p. Index, pp. 235-43.

Essays, by researchers in the social sciences, examine the models,
methods, and data in the field of social area analysis. Among
the topics which are included are housing supply and market behavior, household location, and spatial form in the residential
mosaic.

Hirsch, Werner Z., ed. URBAN LIFE AND FORM. New York: Holt, Rinehart and Winston, 1963. 248 p. Notes, pp. 246-48.

This collection of papers resulting from a faculty seminar at the Institute for Urban and Regional Studies at Washington University deal with perspectives and foundations of urban form. The emergence of urban form, "The City in History," government, political science, and planning are among the topics covered. Contributors include: W. Hirsch, R. Wade, R. Wood, L. Schnore, and S. Chapin.

Hochman, Harold M., ed. THE URBAN ECONOMY. New York: W.W. Norton, 1976. 296 p. Suggested Further Reading, pp. 94-96. No index.

Reprints of articles by K. Davis, E. Mills, R. Dorfman, D. Netzer, W. Baumol, W. Oattes, W. Thompson, B. Chinitz, R. Bish, J. Kain, J. Forrester, W. Alonso, A. Downs, J. Bergsman, and A. Brimmer are included in this readings book. It is organized into five parts which systematically cover "Urban Structure and Functions," "Urban Finance and Government," "The Economy of the Central City," "The Future of the Inner City," and the "Urban Crisis and Urban Prospect."

Hughes, James W., ed. SURURBANIZATION DYNAMICS AND THE FUTURE OF THE CITY. New Brunswick, N.J.: Rutgers University Press, 1974. 300 p. Index.

The process of suburbanization is examined in this collection of essays, and the components of the process are analyzed.

James, Franklin J., ed. MODELS OF EMPLOYMENT AND RESIDENCE LOCATION. New Brunswick, N.J.: Center for Urban Policy Research, Rutgers University, 1974. 399 p.

Written for and by economists, this work contains 15 essays, addresses, lectures, and others on areas of jobs in metropolitan areas, households in metropolitan areas, applied models and the theory of urban housing, job location, and wages. Some of the authors whose works are included are: J.F. Kain, R.F. Muth, I.S. Lowry, F.S. Chapin and S.F. Weiss, F. deLeeuw, and L.N.Moses.

Johnson, James H., ed. SUBURBAN GROWTH: GEOGRAPHICAL PROCESSES AT THE EDGE OF A WESTERN CITY. New York: John Wiley and Sons, 1974. xv, 257 p. Index, pp. 249-57.

This is a group of eleven essays devoted to a geographic approach to suburban expansion. Of specific interest is the interaction between the rural and urban areas at the urban fringe.

Kain, John F., ed. ESSAYS ON URBAN SPATIAL STRUCTURE. Cambridge, Mass.: Ballinger Publishing Co., 1975. 412 p. Notes, pp. 363-406. Index, pp. 407-10.

This is a collection of 17 essays dealing with a wide range of research on questions involving urban space. Urban economic and policy discussions are included, and an extensive introduction traces the development of urban economics and links the remaining essays. Major topic headings include: "Residential and Commuting Decisions," "The Location of Jobs," "Effects of Racial Discrimination," "Analysis of Urban Housing Markets," and "Urban Transportation."

Kramer, Simon Pail, ed. THE CITY IN AMERICAN LIFE, A HISTORICAL ANTHOLOGY. New York: G.P. Putman, 1970.

Leahy, W.H.; McKee, D.L.; and Dean, R.D., eds. URBAN ECONOMICS: THEORY, DEVELOPMENT AND PLANNING. New York: Free Press, 1970. viii, 339 p.

Leven, Charles L., ed. THE MATURE METROPOLIS. Lexington, Mass.: Lexington Books, 1978. x, 317 p. No index.

This group of essays examines post World War II growth trends in order to better understand the process of urbanization and the situation of the mature metropolis. The volume contains seven parts: "Introduction," "Overview," "Origin of Maturity," "Functions of the Mature Metropolis," "Physical Origins of the Mature Metropolis," "Government Origins and the Mature Metropolis," and "Private, Public and Human Investment in the Mature Metropolis." There are contributions by: C. Leven, W. Alonso, J. Coleman, P. Hall, H. Perloff, E. Mills, L. Moses, A. Campbell, A. Downs, D. Netzer, H. Richardson, and R. Holland.

Levin, Melvin R., ed. EXPLORING URBAN PROBLEMS. Boston: Urban Press, 1971. xxiii, 667 p. No index.

This is an introductory "hybrid" book which examines the unmet needs of urban areas. Urban problems is the theme, and various authors explore different attitudes toward these problems. The book is divided into five parts. Part I is devoted to "The Urban Planners Trinity: Population, Land Use, Economic Base." "The Physical Structure of Urban Areas" is the topic of part II. Part III discusses "Social Problems and Progress," with particular focus on education, poverty, race, and crime. Urban government and finance is covered in part IV and part V looks at the future of urban areas. Contributors include: W. Thompson, J. Meyer, and D. Netzer.

Lewis, Jordan D., and Lynn, Lewis, eds. INDUSTRIAL APPROACHES TO URBAN PROBLEMS, DISCUSSIONS OF HOUSING, TRANSPORTATION, EDUCATION AND SOLID WASTE MANAGEMENT ISSUES. New York: Praeger, 1972. xx, 205 p. Index, pp. 185-205.

> This is an analysis of the stated problem areas with suggestions to aid and alleviate them. The solutions are made from a technical perspective.

Lineberry, Robet L., and Masotti, Louis H., eds. URBAN PROBLEMS AND PUBLIC POLICY. Lexington, Mass.: Lexington Books, 1975. xv, 209 p. Index, pp. 205-06.

> The fifteen chapters in this volume of public policy studies examine "The Politics of Policy Change," "Urbanization, Metropolitanism and Policy," "Changing Foci of the Policy Making System," and "The Federalization of Urban Policy." Specific topics examined include transportation, revenue sharing, federal aid, and land use regulation.

Lithwick, N.H., and Paquet, Gilles, eds. URBAN STUDIES: A CANADIAN PERSPECTIVE. Toronto: Methuen, 1968. ix, 290 p. Bibliography, pp. 275-80. Index, pp. 281-90.

> This is a cross-disciplinary approach to the urban area with a heavy dose of economics. Regional economics and land use is covered, case studies are introduced, and public policies for urban and regional areas are discussed. This volume is for economists, political scientists, sociologists, and geographers.

Lowenstein, Louis K., ed. URBAN STUDIES: AN INTRODUCTORY READER. New York: Free Press, 1977. xxii, 488 p. Index, pp. 482-88.

> These twenty essays deal with subjects ranging from the form and structure of urban areas to issues such as poverty, education, urban finances, education, and the urban environment. Readability and an understanding of current trends was the key to selection.

McKenon, James E., ed. THE CHANGING METROPOLIS. Boston: Houghton Mifflin, 1971.

McMaster, J.C., and Webb, G.R., eds. AUSTRALIAN URBAN ECONOMICS. Sidney: Australia and New Zealand Book Co., 1976. xi, 595 p. Bibliography, pp. 585-88. Author Index, pp. 589-93. Subject Index, pp. 593-95. Illus.

> This is a readings text for a course in urban economics with Australian examples and perspectives. There is a particular interest in a worldwide application of economic analysis to urban and regional problems rather than a U.S.-U.K. emphasis. The 27 readings are divided into seven topic areas. They are: "National

Urban Strategy" (one essay), "Urban Land Policy" (three essays), "Urban Growth and the Process of Urban Development" (five essays), "Public Utilities for Urban Development" (three essays), "Housing and Urban Renewal" (five essays), "Decentralization, Regional Development and the Case for New Cities" (eight essays), and "Urban and Regional Finance" (two essays). W. Alonso and G. Neutze are contributors.

Mass, Nathaniel J., ed. READINGS IN URBAN DYNAMICS. Vol. I. Cambridge, Mass.: Wright-Allen Press, 1974. x, 303 p.

This volume offers more on the systems approach for those interested in economic modeling based on Jay Forrester's URBAN DYNAMICS. There is a greater emphasis placed on viewpoints and methodology here than in the original. Business structure and activity, underemployment, migration, policy and design, and modeling the city-suburb are among the topics covered. It is a systems methodology and framework for economists interested in this type of tool for policy and research design.

Mayer, Harold M., and Kohn, Clide F. READINGS IN URBAN GEOGRAPHY. Chicago: University of Chicago Press, 1959. vii, 625 p. Index of Authors, pp. 605-08. Index of Subjects, pp. 609-25.

While this reader was designed for use by urban geographers, many of the 55 essays are of interest to economists and students of urban economics. There are 18 sections in the book, and those relevant to economists include: "Basic Definitions--SMSA's," "The Rise and Growth of Cities," "The Economic Base of Cities," "Classification of Cities," "Urban Population Studies," "Cities as Central Places," "Size and Spacing of Cities," "General Nature of City Structure," "Transportation," and the "Commercial," "Industrial," and "Residential Structure of Cities."

Meadows, Paul, and Mirzuchi, Emphraim H., eds. URBANISM, URBANIZATION AND CHANGE: COMPARATIVE PERSPECTIVES. Reading, Mass.: Addison-Wesley Publishing Co., 1969. 579 p. Author Index, pp. 575-76. Subject Index, pp. 577-79.

These are interdisciplinary readings for students of urban sociology, urban studies, and others. The focus is on urbanization and social change. Economists might have a passing interest in the work.

Mesarovic, Michaglo D., and Reisman, Arnold, eds. SYSTEMS APPROACH AND THE CITY. Amsterdam: North Holland Publishing Co., 1972.

This collection is a summary of the proceedings of a symposium at Case Western Reserve dealing with a focus on the concept and methodology of urban systems. Many of the essays are inquiries into the systems approach and take specific looks at health, air, water, transportation, and traffic systems.

Meyerson, Martin, ed. THE CONSCIENCE OF THE CITY. New York: Braziller, 1970. xv, 412 p. Index, p. 397.

This volume offers a social science approach to the traditional city in transition, the process of change, and the goals for change. The shifting of priorities and emphasis on certain programs is examined as well.

Miles, Simon R., ed. METROPOLITAN PROBLEMS, INTERNATIONAL PROSPECTS, A SEARCH FOR COMPREHENSIVE SOLUTIONS. Toronto: Methuen, 1970. xv, 554 p. Index, pp. 529-54.

This series of papers commissioned by the Canadian government for use in training programs on urban problems provides a diversified collection of issues and approaches to most common metropolitan problem areas. The 15 selections are divided into four parts: "The Contemporary Metropolis," "Service in Metropolitan Areas," "Developing a Governmental Machinery," and "A Contemporary Metropolis." The approach taken is "holistic."

Mohl, Raymond A., ed. URBAN AMERICA IN HISTORICAL PERSPECTIVE. New York: Weybright and Tally, 1970. 426 p.

Moore, Eric G., ed. MODELS OF RESIDENTIAL LOCATION AND RELOCATION IN THE CITY. Northwestern University Studies in Geography, no. 20. Evanston, Ill.: Northwestern University Press, 1973. 199 p.

This volume contains six essays by Menchuk, Straszhem, Ginsberg, Golant, Moore, Gale, and Ginsberg and generate location models in an urban context.

Page, Alfred N., and Seyfried, Warren R., eds. URBAN ANALYSIS: READINGS IN HOUSING AND URBAN DEVELOPMENT. Glenview, Ill.: Scott, Foresman and Co., 1970. 427 p. No index.

These readings focus on the "important economic aspects of the role of housing in urban development." Five major sections include: "Housing and the Urban Environment" (four essays), "Economic Analysis of Urban Housing Demand" (seven essays), "Housing and Intra-Urban Location" (eight essays), "Urban Housing and Racial Integration" (seven essays), and "Slums, Urban Renewal and Public Policy" (nine essays). Contributors include: J. Spengler, B. Harris, J. Guttentag, R. Muth, W. Alonso, L. Wingo, J. Kain, B. Duncan and O.D. Duncan, C. Tiebout, G. Sternlieb, and I. Loury. Both theoretical and empirical essays are found in this collection.

Pascal, Anthony H., ed. THINKING ABOUT CITIES, NEW PERSPECTIVES ON URBAN PROBLEMS. Belmont, Calif.: Dickenson Publishing Co., 1970. x, 185 p. Index, pp. 179-85.

This volume contains essays by R. Dorfman, K. Arrow, L. Thurow, N. Glazer, S. Lipset, A. Pascal, I. Kristol, and J. Margolis on topics of race relations, institutional functions of cities, manpower, poverty, human resource exploitation, violence, and other welfare-type issues. The work sprang from a workshop of social scientists at Rand Corporation. The papers vary in the depth of treatment and in focus. They range from the historical to the analytical.

Perloff, Harvey S., ed. THE QUALITY OF THE URBAN ENVIRONMENT: ESSAYS ON "NEW RESOURCES" IN AN URBAN AGE. Baltimore: Johns Hopkins University Press for Resources for the Future, 1969. xii, 344 p. No index.

These nine essays stem from a conference on the urban environment held by R.F.F. to review the "state of the art" and to "stimulate research." Participants were asked to review the established concepts and information as well as those which were evolving and those needed to advance the field and to review public policy issues. There is a mix of theoretical, conceptual, empirical, and observational essays. Contributors include: H. Perloff, I. Hoch, M. Clawson, E. Mills, B.J.L. Berry, F.S. Chapin, and T. Logan.

Perloff, Harvey S., and Nathan, Richard P., eds. REVENUE SHARING AND THE CITY. Baltimore: Johns Hopkins Press for Resources for the Future, 1968. x, 122 p.

There are two papers included, discussed, and rebuted in this book. The major authors are W. Heller and E. Ruggles.

Perloff, Harvey S., and Wingo, Lowdon, Jr., eds. ISSUES IN URBAN ECONOMICS. Baltimore: Johns Hopkins University Press for Resources for the Future, 1968. x, 668 p. Paper. Subject Index, pp. 651-62. Name Index, pp. 663-68.

These readings stem from papers presented at a conference sponsored by the Committee on Urban Economics of R.F.F. The mission of this conference was to establish "benchmarks" in the field of urban economics. In each of the 12 articles, authors were asked "to describe the range of problems" in the chosen area and "to synthesize the results so far and the challenges ahead." The contents of this volume follows:

Part I--"The Urban Economy within the National Economy," "Internal and External Factors in the Development of Urban Economics" by W. Thompson, "The Evolving System of Cities in the U.S." by E. Lampard, "The Uses and Development of Regional Projections" by S. Sonenblum, and "The Changing Profile of Human Resources" by G. Stolnitz.

Part II--"Intra Metropolitan Development," "The Evolving Form and Organization of the Metropolis" by E. Hoover, "Urban Residential Land and Housing Markets" by R. Muth, "Poverty in the Cities" by O. Ornati, and "Quantitative Modes of Urban

Development" by B. Harris.
Part III--"The Urban Public Economy," "Federal, State, and Local Finance in a Metropolitan Context" by D. Netzer, "The Supply of Urban Public Services" by W. Hirsch, and "The Demand for Urban Public Services" by J. Margolis.
Part IV--"Policy Issues," "Public Policy for Urban America" by J. Burkhead and A. Campbell.

Popenoe, David. THE URBAN INDUSTRIAL FRONTIER: ESSAYS ON SOCIAL TRENDS AND INSTITUTIONAL GOALS IN MODERN COMMUNITIES. New Brunswick, N.J.: Rutgers University Press, 1969. xiv, 177 p. No index.

In this volume eleven essays appear under the broad headings of the city in urban-industrial society, institutional goals and trends in urban-industrial communities, and some larger contexts of community institutions. The essays are a mixture of normative and empirical work and are aimed at urban social planners.

Portney, Paul R., ed. ECONOMIC ISSUES IN METROPOLITAN GROWTH. Baltimore: Johns Hopkins University Press, 1976. x, 143 p.

These papers were originally presented at a forum conducted by Resources for the Future in May, 1975 in Washington, D.C. They are: "Fiscal Impact Studies in a Metropolitan Context" by T. Ellman, "Property Value Maximization as a Criteria for Local Government" by J. Sonstelie and P. Portney, "Metropolitan Growth and the Public Utilities" by M. Sharefkin, "Taxes on Land Development" by B. Schechter, and "Local Government Finance and the Regulated Firm" by J.M. Cummens.

Powell, J.M., ed. URBAN AND INDUSTRIAL AUSTRALIA: READINGS IN HUMAN GEOGRAPHY. Melbourne: Sorrett Publishing, 1972. 252 p. Bibliographical references, graphs, maps, tables.

Primarily for students of geography, this book examines the city in terms of the industry in the city, the internal structure, and retailing. The city is also examined in its regional setting and as part of a system. Australian cities are used as examples for the discussion.

Pynoos, Jon; Schafer, Robert; and Hartman, Chester W., eds. HOUSING URBAN AMERICA. Chicago: Aldine, 1973. 690 p.

This is an anthology of the current literature on urban housing. The five sections on "Politics," "Social Aspects," "Economics," "Production," and "Policies and Programs" contain 50 essays, several of which were written specifically for this collection. There is a balance of theoretical, empirical, and policy essays, and the first four parts are preceeded by introductions which link the essays and put the discussion into perspective.

Rasmussen, David., and Haworth, Charles T. THE MODERN CITY: READINGS IN URBAN ECONOMICS. New York: Harper and Row, 1973. x, 302 p. Index, pp. 297-302.

The urban problem areas included in this group of readings are housing and urban renewal, transportation, the urban public economy, and population distribution. Sections are also devoted to the urbanization process, income distribution, and location. These reprinted articles include work by J. Wilson, E. Hoover, G. Sternlieb, R. Sherman, W. Vickrey, J. Meyer, and N. Hansen. There is a companion text by these authors.

Rodwin, Lloyd, ed. THE FUTURE METROPOLIS. New York: George Braziller, 1960. 253 p.

These 12 essays were originally published in DAEDALUS, the journal of the American Academy of Arts and Sciences in the winter of 1961. Authors include: R. Vernon, E. Banfield, K. Lynch, and L. Rodwin.

Rosenbloom, Richard S., and Marris, Robin, eds. SOCIAL INNOVATION IN THE CITY, NEW ENTERPRISES FOR COMMUNITY DEVELOPMENT. Working papers. Cambridge: Harvard University Press, 1969. xi, 200 p.

This collection of papers represents an interim work being done in the relation of the city to technical advances. Topic areas covered include transportation, economics, housing, poverty, and, among others, welfare.

Rothblatt, Donald N., ed. NATIONAL POLICY FOR METROPOLITAN AND REGIONAL DEVELOPMENT. Lexington, Mass.: Lexington Books, 1974. 224 p. Notes, tables, figures, bibliography.

The essays in this volume "provided a comprehensive framework for evaluating the opportunities for establishing a national urban and regional development policy in the United States." Several analytical approaches, such as rationality models, incrementalism, gaming, and cost-benefit analysis are used to explain and evaluate the public policy-making process. European regional policies are elaborated and compared to those of the United States. A discussion of goals for future policies concludes the work.

Schnore, Leo F., ed. SOCIAL SCIENCE AND THE CITY: A SURVEY OF URBAN RESEARCH. New York: Praeger, 1967. 335 p. Bibliography, pp. 303-35.

These studies examine the priorities of many of the disciplines of the social sciences toward the city. Most of the essays are empirical and geared toward research based on urban policy. Two of the ten essays are directed toward economics and regional science. They are: "Toward an Urban Economics" by W. Thompson and "Urban Travel Behavior" by J. Kain.

Schreiber, Arthur F.; Gatons, Paul K.; and Clemmer, Richard B. ECONOMICS OF URBAN PROBLEMS: SELECTED READINGS. New York: Houghton Mifflin, 1971. 278 p. No index.

> These 15 readings are reprints of articles and are of value to economists as well as noneconomists. The collection is recommended for use as a supplementary text in a variety of courses. The four major topic areas covered are: "Efficiency, Equity and Urban Problems," "Poverty and Housing," "Transportation and Pollution," and "Financing Urban Public Services." Each section has a major introduction. Authors whose work is reprinted include: J. Meyer, J. Kain, M. Wohl, D. Netzer, W. Heller, and J. Pechman. These authors have published a companion textbook.

Schroeder, Walter W. III; Sweeney, Robert E.; and Alfeld, Louis Edward, eds. READINGS IN URBAN DYNAMICS. Vol. 2. Cambridge, Mass.: Wright-Allen Press, 1975. 305 p. Index, pp. 303-5.

> This group of essays is the second round of discussion relating to Jay Forrester's URBAN DYNAMICS. They were generated from a research program established to extend and respond to issues in urban modeling. The 12 essays cover a variety of topics from migration and housing availability to the use of data in modeling. Contributors include: J. Forrester, W. Schroeder, A. Makowski, P. Senge, J.S. Miller, and L.E. Alfeld.

Schwirian, Kent P., ed. COMPARATIVE URBAN STRUCTURE: STUDIES IN THE ECOLOGY OF CITIES. Lexington, Mass.: D.C. Heath, 1974. xiii, 603 p. References, pp. 602-03.

> Some fifty essays are brought together in this collection. Most are relatively recent and are useful to students of urban structure. Designed for use as a text, the readings examine general urban models, population density models, the general organization of space, factorial ecology, and social area analysis. Contributors include B. Duncan, L. Schnore, B.J.L. Berry, C. Harris, and O.D. Duncan.

Soen, Dan, ed. URBAN RENEWAL: AN INTERDISCIPLINARY SYMPOSIUM. Tel Aviv: Institute for Planning and Development, 1968. 259 p. Paper. No index.

> There are four of the 15 papers in this volume that deal with economic aspects of the Israeli experience with urban renewal. They are: "Economic Implications of Slum Rehabilitation Plans in Israel," "The Systems Approach Applied to Urban Rehabilitation," "The Use of Cost-Benefit Analysis in Urban Renewal Planning," and "The Tel Aviv Master Plan, Land Prices and the Problem of Slum Rehabilitation."

Spreiregen, Paul D., ed. METROPOLIS AND BEYOND: SELECTED ESSAYS BY HANS BLUMENFELD. New York: John Wiley and Sons, 1979. xiii, 420 p. Subject Index, pp. 411-18. Geographical Index, pp. 419-20.

> This is a unique view of the metropolis from this architect who has scoured the literature of the urban world. Several of the 45 essays might be of interest to urban economists, including those in the sections on "Economics" (four), "Housing" (eight), "Transportation" (eight), and "Prospects" (four).

Sternlieb, George, and Hughes, James W., eds. POST-INDUSTRIAL AMERICA: METROPOLITAN DECLINE AND INTERREGIONAL JOB SHIFTS. New Brunswick, N.J.: Rutgers University, Center for Urban Policy Research, 1975. 267 p. No index.

> This group of papers is the result of a conference held to examine the impact of shifts in the economy. A lengthy prologue sets the stage for the essays on "The Trendlines and Patterns of Change," and the "Underlying Processes and Problems." Contributors include: M. Greenberg, G. Sternlieb, B.J.L. Berry, W. Thompson, J. Kain, N. Glazer, and R. Starr.

Stearns, Forest, and Montag, Tom, eds. THE URBAN ECOSYSTEM: A HOLISTIC APPROACH. Stroudsburg, Pa.: Dowden, Hutchinson and Ross, 1975. xv, 217 p.

> This is a collection of essays in the "work of 90 specialists from the natural and social sciences . . . to correlate and integrate existing work into a framework for future study."

Sweeney, Stephen B., ed. METROPOLITAN ANALYSIS, IMPORTANT ELEMENTS IN STUDY AND ACTION. Philadelphia: University of Pennsylvania, 1958. 189 p. No index.

> This work is the result of a workshop for government officials and citizens of the metropolitan area where approaches to metropolitan problems and studies of the metropolitan area were discussed. There is a heavy emphasis on examination of the economic structure of metropolitan areas.

Sweet, David C., ed. MODELS OF URBAN STRUCTURE. Lexington, Mass.: Lexington Books, 1972. 288 p. Figures and tables.

> These papers are the result of a symposium where the specified task was to identify the needs in the "development of models for analyzing the problems of urban structure." There are contributions from economists, geographers, regional scientists, urban planners, and sociologists. The twelve essays fit into two major headings: "Application of Urban-Structure Models" and "New Concepts in Urban-Structure Models."

Tabb, William K., and Sawers, Larry, eds. MARXISM AND THE METROPOLIS: NEW PERSPECTIVES IN URBAN POLITICAL ECONOMY. New York: Oxford University Press, 1978. viii, 376 p. Index, pp. 368-76.

The papers included in this collection resulted from a conference held at the New School for Social Research. Participants were frustrated by the inability of disciplinary tools to deal with urban problems. All essays "owe a heavy debt to Marx and Engles." Part I looks "From City to Metropolis" and contains articles by D. Gordon, P. Ashton, and A. Markusen. "Construction and Destruction: Urban Redevelopment" is the subject of part II and includes the work of J. Mollenkopf, R. Kessler, and M. Stone. "The Buck Stops Here" includes reviews of urban fiscal problems by R. Hill and W. Tabb. Part IV, "Urbanizing to Meet the Challenge" contains contributions by O. Green and A. Hunter and K. Coit. "Learning from Others: Cities and Socialism" is the topic of part V. D. Barkin examines the Cuban situation, and L. Sawers looks at the Soviet Union and China.

Urban Economic Conference, 2d University of Keel, 1973. PAPERS. 2 vols. London: Center for Environmental Studies, 1974. 301 p.

Volume 1 is devoted to issues concerning reform of housing, finance, externalities, a micro analysis of the urban housing market, and thoughts on the economies of intraurban spatial location.

Volume 2 concerns issues such as factors explaining the size distribution of family income in U.S. SMSAs, location decisions from past moves, land prices, and the urban land market policy.

Vance, Rupert B., and Demerath, Nicholas J., ed. THE URBAN SOUTH. Chapel Hill: University of North Carolina Press, 1954. xii, 307 p.

These are studies in regionalism and urbanism in the South. An underlying theme running through these essays is the breakthrough in the regions' position as correlated with growing urbanization. The organizational aspects of urbanization, regional change, and tradition are topics of the individual papers.

Venetoulis, Theodore, and Eisenhauer, Ward, eds. UP AGAINST THE URBAN WALL. Englewood Cliffs, N.J.: Prentice-Hall, 1971. xiv, 546 p. Index, pp. 543-46.

These 45 readings tend to be of a general social science nature. Topic areas include: "The Urban Concepts," "The Urban Condition," "The Brutality of Urban Politics," "Scars of Urban Alienation," "America's Response to the Urban Crisis," and "Towards a New Urban America." L. Rainwater, J. Lindsay, N. Glazer, E. Banfield, J. Jacobs, and W. Heller are among the contributors.

Walton, John, and Masotti, Louis, eds. THE CITY IN COMPARATIVE PER-
SPECTIVE: CROSS-SECTIONAL RESEARCH AND NEW DIRECTIONS IN THEORY.
New York: John Wiley and Sons, 1976. x, 317 p. No index.

The editors have put together a collection of readings which examine a new subfield in the social sciences--that of comparative
urban research. These essays attempt to define a body of theory
and a unified methodology for this subfield. Contributors repre-
sent many disciplines, and the essays are divided into five major
parts. Part I gives a general introduction to comparative urban
research. Part II discusses the "Theory and Method in Comparative Urban Economy. Parts III and IV examine "The City in Developing Societies," and part V searches for "New Directions in
Theory."

Warner, Sam Bass, Jr., ed. PLANNING FOR A NATION OF CITIES. Cambridge: M.I.T. Press, 1966. ix, 310 p.

These essays examine the need for planning in urban America in
terms of the federal responsibility, the funds needed, the quality
of life, the role of the suburbs, and metropolitan services.

Whithed, Marshall H., ed., and Sorly, Robert M., associate ed. URBAN
SIMULATION: MODELS FOR PUBLIC POLICY. Leiden, Netherlands: Sijthoff
International Publishing Co., 1974. xi, 282 p.

These papers were first presented at the Advanced Studies Institute
of Urban Simulation Analyses and Modeling in London in 1973 and
were revised for publication in this volume. The focus is on the
usefulness of these techniques in the urban decision-making process.
The four parts of the book are: applications to comprehensive urban
development, applications in urban management, specialized applications of urban simulation analysis, and interactive simulation and
simulation gaming.

Wilson, James Q., ed. THE METROPOLITAN ENIGMA. Garden City, N.Y.:
Doubleday and Co., 1968. x, 392 p. Index, pp. 377-92.

This is the Harvard-M.I.T. Joint Center for Urban Studies response
to a request by the U.S. Chamber of Commerce to prepare a series
of papers on urban problems. This revised and expanded version of
a 1967 publication by the Joint Center contains 12 essays which
attempt to "disentangle and analyze the various problems." A
distinction is also made between "urban problems" and those that
are to be found in an urban nation. The following essays are
included: "The Distribution and Movement of Jobs and Industry"
by J. Kain, "Urban Transportation" by J. Meyer, "Financing
Urban Government" by D. Netzer, "Pollution and Cities" by R.
Revelle, "Race and Migration in the American City" by C. Tilly,
"Housing and National Urban Goals" by B. Frieden, "Design and
Urban Beauty in the Central City" by J. Burchard, "Urban Crime"

by M. Wolfgang, "Rioting for Fun" by E. Banfield, "The Schools in the City" by T. Sizer, "Poverty in Cities" by D. Moynihan, and "Urban Problems in Perspective" by J. Wilson.

Wingo, Lowdon, Jr., ed. CITIES AND SPACE. THE FUTURE USE OF URBAN LAND. Baltimore: Johns Hopkins Press for Resources for the Future, 1963. 261 p. Index, pp. 251-61.

This collection of essays addresses "the urban problem," given legal, political, cultural and economic constraints. The essays included are: "Urban Space in a Policy Perspective" by L. Wingo, "Order in Diversity: Community without Propinquity" by M. Webber, "The Importance of Open Space in the Urban Pattern" by S. Tankel, "The Form and Structure of the Future Urban Complex" by Catherine Bauer Wurster, "Urban Space and Urban Design" by F. Gutheim, "The Human Measure: Man and Family in Megalopolis" by L. Duhl, "Public Policy and the Space Economy of the City" by R. Artle, "The Social Control of Urban Space" by C. Haar, and "Social Foresight and the Use of Urban Space" by H. Fagin.

Wright, W.D.C., and Steward, D.H., eds. THE EXPANDING CITY. Edinburgh: University Press, 1972. 189 p. No index.

This is a collection of papers from a seminar on "Urban Growth and the Social Sciences" held at the University of Edinburgh in 1968. The aim was to produce a multidisciplinary approach. Thus, there are sections in the areas of sociology, economics, geography, politics, and urban transportation. Economists contributing are: P.A. Stone, J.N. Wolfe, and J.P. Lewis.

Yin, Robert K., ed. THE CITY IN THE SEVENTIES. Itasca, Ill.: F.E. Peacock Publishers, 1972. xvii, 285 p. Name Index, pp. 273-76. Subject Index, pp. 277-85.

Yin has pulled together research themes which he feels will be important over the next few years. It is a multidisciplinary collection, with those in the first section examining the various "Components of the City." Section II looks at the "Study of the City," and Section III focuses on "A Glimpse of the Future." There are 37 readings in this collection.

Chapter 8

URBAN ECONOMICS TEXTS

Asterisks preceding entries denote readings books which are annotated in chapter 7. They were designed to be used with or without textbooks.

Bish, Robert L., and Kirk, Robert J. ECONOMIC PRINCIPLES AND URBAN PROBLEMS. Englewood Cliffs, N.J.: Prentice Hall, 1974. viii, 199 p. Index, pp. 195–99.

> The focus of this text is on market forces and how they shape and influence urban areas. Demand, supply, scarcity, resource allocation, and other economic principles are used to analyze urban problems and concerns. The book's 14 chapters are divided into four main parts: "The Market System in Urban Areas," "The Failures of the Market System," "Government in Urban Areas," and "Economic Analysis of Urban Problems." The examples of market failures which are used are pollution and income distribution by race. Urban problems which are examined are transportation, housing and urban renewal, and education. The authors suggest this book for introductory economics courses.

Bish, Robert L., and Nourse, Hugh O. URBAN ECONOMICS AND POLICY ANALYSIS. New York: McGraw-Hill, 1975. v, 435 p. Index, pp. 427–35.

> In this text, microeconomics and location theory are integrated with public choice theory to provide the foundation for a fairly comprehensive view of urban economics. The text begins with a historical examination of urbanization through the industrial revolution and the rise of the market system. Theory is then integrated into an analysis of urban problems. The thirteen chapters cover: "Urbanization, Location and Growth," "Urban Land Use, Public Goods and Political Organization," "Urban Public Finance," "Issues in Public Sector Organization," "Housing Segregation," "Zoning and Land Use Control," "The Urban Environment," "Transportation," and "The Future." A summary and selected readings conclude each chapter.

Bollen, John C., and Schmandt, Henry J. THE METROPOLIS: ITS PEOPLE, POLITICS AND ECONOMIC LIFE. New York: Harper and Row, 1970. x, 488 p. A Commentary on Bibliography, pp. 447-64. Index of Names, pp. 465-72. Index of Subjects, pp. 473-88.

> The sixteen chapters in this text cover a wide variety of issues in urban life, ranging from the city as an economic unit and a geographical area to the social and governmental systems within the city. The purpose of the authors was to "present a balanced multidimensional view of the metropolis with an emphasis on process and behavior, form and structure." Thus, there are discussions of social characteristics and trends in urban areas, economic development, land use considerations, urban politics, and government and citizen roles. The bibliographical essays at the end are quite comprehensive.

Brown, Douglas M. INTRODUCTION TO URBAN ECONOMICS. New York: Academic Press, 1974. ix, 301 p.

> This is a principles of urban economics text which discusses the nature and function of cities, the U.S. experience since 1600, growth, location theory, and a traditional treatment of urban problem areas.

Button, K.J. URBAN ECONOMICS: THEORY AND POLICY. London: Macmillan Co., 1976. iv, 218 p. Index, pp. 211-18. Bibliographies at the end of each chapter.

> This text grew out of an urban economics course in the United Kingdom for senior and postgraduate students. The approach is nonmathematical, and only a limited knowledge of economic theory is necessary. In addition to economics, social, political, planning, and geographical perspectives of the urban process are considered. The book takes a "problem solving approach" to urban-oriented questions.

Durr, Fred. THE URBAN ECONOMY. Scranton, Pa.: Intext Educational Publishers, 1971. xiii, 201 p. Bibliography, pp. 195-98. Index, pp. 199-201.

> Economic factors which operate in cities are reviewed in the process of finding solutions. Issues of both national and local interest are used to illustrate and apply elementary economic concepts. Topic areas include: fluctuation in the urban economy, urban land and land economics, urban demography, transportation, and finance, income and consumption in urban areas, demands for urban services, and the urban future.

*Edel, Mathew, and Rothenberg, Jerome, eds. READINGS IN URBAN ECONOMICS. New York: Macmillan Co., 1972. vi, 602 p. No index.

Emerson, M. Jarvin, and Lamphear, F. Charles. URBAN AND REGIONAL ECONOMICS. Boston: Allyn and Bacon, 1975. viii, 360 p. Index, pp. 345-60.

Both regional and urban economics are integrated into this text which recommends an introductory economics course as a prerequisite. The authors integrate the materials and problems which are similar for the two areas and provide an analytical framework to examine particular problem areas. The eighteen chapters are divided equally among urban and regional topics. The chapters on regional economics are devoted to examinations of the regional industrial structure, performance, location analysis, spatial competition, pricing and location, city size distribution and central place analysis, regional structure and growth, interregional trade, and factor flows. Urban structures are examined descriptively and theoretically with attention then given to the problem areas of urban public finance, poverty and housing, transportation and pollution, government and land use, and new towns and the urban future. Theory, problems, and policy are spread throughout, and analytical techniques are interspersed.

Frieden, Bernard J., and Nash, William W., Jr., eds. SHAPING AN URBAN FUTURE: ESSAYS IN MEMORY OF CATHERINE BAUER WURSTER. Cambridge: M.I.T. Press, 1969.

Geruson, Richard T., and McGrath, Dennis. CITIES AND URBANIZATION. New York: Praeger, 1977. xviii, 233 p. Selected References, pp. 207-22. Index, pp. 223-33.

The unusual feature of this historically oriented text is that it is the joint approach and work of an economist and a sociologist. From their combined viewpoints, they examine the nature of the city and the process of urbanization. Three critical functions of cities are emphasized: the interactive, the generative, and the upgrading. The nature and origin of cities are examined, as is the emergence of the industrial city. Chapters 2 through 8 trace the development of the modern city and examine the forces which have shaped the city of today.

Goodall, Brian. THE ECONOMICS OF URBAN AREAS. Urban and Regional Planning Series, vol. 3. New York: Pergamon Press, 1972. xii, 379 p. Index, pp. 376-79.

This general introduction to the urban economy is designed for beginning students and laypeople. The book includes discussions of the urban economic base, urban property markets, location decisions of business and households, urban growth, and urban government.

*Gordon, David M., ed. PROBLEMS IN POLITICAL ECONOMY: AN URBAN PERSPECTIVE. 2d ed. Lexington, Mass.: D.C. Heath, 1977. xvi, 528 p. No index.

*Greenberg, Michael R., ed. READINGS IN URBAN ECONOMICS AND SPATIAL PATTERNS. New Brunswick, N.J.: Center for Urban Policy Research, Rutgers University, 1974. 328 p. Supplementary bibliography, pp. 319-28.

Grieson, Ronald E., ed. URBAN ECONOMICS: READINGS AND ANALYSIS. Boston: Little, Brown and Co., 1973. x, 453 p.

Heilbrun, James. URBAN ECONOMICS AND PUBLIC POLICY. New York: St. Martin's Press, 1974. xviii, 380 p. Index, pp. 367-80.

The analytical tools of economics are again used to explain the spatial and economics organization of cities and to focus on particular problems. The author recommends an introductory economics and high school algebra as requisites, though the approach is nonmathematical. The thirteen chapters include discussions of the scope of urban economics and the economics of urbanization; the growth of cities and location of economic activity; the system of cities and the urban hierarchy; land use patterns, transportation and urban form; the economic base and policy; poverty and antipoverty policies; housing problems and policies; and the problems of urban finance. A postscript deals with the problems of urban decline and growth.

Henderson, William L., and Ledebur, Larry C. URBAN ECONOMICS: PROCESSES AND PROBLEMS. New York: John Wiley and Sons, 1972. xix, 216 p. Index, pp. 213-16.

This text is divided into two basic parts: the processes of the urban economy and the problems. The section on urban economic processes deals with history and future trends, the structure of economic activity, the economic functions of a city, and the failure of the market as a regulator decision maker. Discussions of urban growth, agglomeration economies, capital markets, and the role of government are included in this part. The urban economic problems discussed in part II include urban public services, transportation, housing, the ghetto, and the dilemma of the future.

Hendon, William Scott. ECONOMICS FOR URBAN SOCIAL PLANNING. Salt Lake City: University of Utah Press, 1975. 314 p. Subject Index, pp. 307-13. Name Index, pp. 313-14. Bibliographical references at end of chapters.

This book is designed for undergraduate economics students or as a supplementary work for senior students or students of urban affairs. It takes a predominately microeconomic approach. The subjects covered include the human resources in the city, urban politics, and an evaluation of urban policies pursued by local governments.

Hirsch, Werner Z. URBAN ECONOMIC ANALYSIS. New York: McGraw-Hill, 1973. xviii, 450 p. Name Index, pp. 443-45. Subject Index, pp. 446-50.

For the advanced undergraduate, this text utilizes both micro and macro theories. After a general introduction, Hirsch delves into micro concerns, externalities, and spatial form. Residential land use and housing is the next topic, followed by an explanation of location models and policy. Demand and supply elements and models of transportation and labor markets are examined before moving into the macro sphere. Export-base, input-output, Key-nesian models, and others are set forth and then applied to the urban framework. Next Hirsch deals with urban growth and stability and the economics of urbanization. There are four chapters devoted to the urban public economy, with a comprehensive chapter on various urban services, urban finance, regulation, and control.

Hordon, Harris E. INTRODUCTION TO URBAN ECONOMICS: ANALYSIS AND POLICY. New York: Appleton-Century-Crofts, 1973. xii, 276 p. Bibliography, pp. 263-70. Index, pp. 271-76.

This is a text in urban economics designed for undergraduates with a focus on the process and evolution of urban problems such as housing, transportation, poverty, pollution, and urban finance. The emphasis is on clarity and readibility in demonstrating the "useful contributions" of economies to urban analysis.

Kohler, Heinz. ECONOMICS AND URBAN PROBLEMS. Lexington, Mass.: D.C. Heath, 1973. x, 470 p. Glossary, pp. 443-55. Index, pp. 457-70.

The approach of this text is to present the basic concepts of use to the students and to deal with various urban problems first from an equity or economic justice perspective and then from an efficiency or allocation perspective. In the last part, urban fiscal policy is discussed. Chapter headings are: "On the Rational Use of Resources," "The Logic of the Market Economy," "The Rise and Fall of the American City," "The Dimensions of Poverty," "On Redistributing Wealth," "Ensuring Good Health," "Providing Skills," "Securing Well Paying Jobs," "Giving Money to the Poor," " The Link Between Poverty and Crime," "The Housing Problem," "The Transportation Problem," and "On the Proper Division of Labor Among Governments." The more technical and theoretical tools of the discipline are "ignored."

*Levin, Melvin R., ed. EXPLORING URBAN PROBLEMS. Boston: Urban Press, 1971. xviii, 667 p. No index.

*Lowenstein, Louis K., ed. URBAN STUDIES: AN INTRODUCTORY READER. New York: Free Press, 1977. xxii, 488 p. Index, pp. 482-88.

Mills, Edwin S. URBAN ECONOMICS. Glenview, Ill.: Scott, Foresman and Co., 1972. v, 277 p. Index, pp. 269-77.

This text discusses Mills's desire to "build a unified thread of analysis useful in the understanding of a variety of urban phenomena and problems." The book is kept short so that readings could be used to supplement the course material. It is intended for use in an upper-division undergraduate course in urban economics. Principles of economics or intermediate micro theory are recommended, as is high school algebra. Calculus is used in one chapter which presents a simple mathematical model of urban structure. The first part of the book (eight chapters) deals with the theory underlying urban economics and the historical trends. Part 2 (chapters 9-14) discusses various urban problems and the public sector. Poverty, housing, slums, urban renewal, urban transportation, local government finances, and pollution are dealt with within the theoretical context developed in part I.

Muth, Richard F. URBAN ECONOMIC PROBLEMS. New York: Harper and Row, 1975. viii, 420 p. Index, pp. 399-420.

This is an elementary text for noneconomics majors which is free of technical analyses. The emphasis is on understanding urban problems in an economic context. Subjects which are covered include: the growth of urban areas, the internal structure of cities, segregation and slums, low income and housing programs, the urban environment, unemployment, education, transfer payments, local taxes, and public expenditures.

Netzer, Dick. ECONOMICS AND URBAN PROBLEMS: DIAGNOSES AND PRESCRIPTIONS. 2d ed. New York: Basic Books, 1974. vii, 275 p. Index, pp. 265-75.

The most serious problem of urban areas are dealt with in this text. Part I examines "The Urban Setting," with an introduction to the urban economy and an overview of the problems. Part II looks at "Policy Options" in terms of dealing with urban poverty, housing markets and policies, urban land use, the urban environment, and transportation. "Raising the Money" is the topic of Part III which discusses urban finances.

Palen, J. John. THE URBAN WORLD. New York: McGraw-Hill, 1975. xv, 495 p. Index, pp. 480-95.

This is a text for courses in urbanism and the structure of cities. A variety of topics are encountered, some of which are rather unusual for an urban text, such as the discussions on ecology, evolution, styles, and power. More traditional areas included are urban renewal, zoning, and planning.

*Perloff, Harvey S., and Wingo, Lowdon, Jr., eds. ISSUES IN URBAN ECONOMICS. Baltimore: Johns Hopkins Press for Resources for the Future, 1968. x, 668 p. Subject Index, pp. 651-62. Name Index, pp. 663-68.

Rasmussen, David W. URBAN ECONOMICS. New York: Harper and Row Publishers, 1973. viii, 196 p. Index, pp. 187-96.

> This text presents an overview of urban economics to undergraduates. Theoretical concepts are introduced early on and are used in discussions involving urban public policy. Regional growth and development is downplayed in favor of a summary of basic urban related issues. Recommended readings conclude each chapter. The ten chapters are organized as follows: "The Urban Crisis," "Economic Theory and the Scope of Urban Economics," "A Profile of the Urban Poor," "National Policies to Combat Urban Poverty," "The Location of Economic Activity and the Survival of the Central Cities," "Housing and Urban Renewal," "The Urban Transportation System," "The Urban Public Sector," "City Size and Consumer Welfare," and "The Urban Future." The companion readings book for this text is cited below.

*Rasmussen, David W., and Haworth, Charles T. THE MODERN CITY: READINGS IN URBAN ECONOMICS. New York: Harper and Row, 1973. v, 302 p. Index, pp. 297-302.

Richardson, Harry W. URBAN ECONOMICS. New York: Dryden Press, 1978. 420 p.

> This is a theoretical approach to the questions of why cities exist, how they grow, and how they change. Location theory is well integrated into the text, as are major urban policy issues. Tools, theories, and models enable the student to analyze the urban sphere. The book contains chapters on "Location and Spatial Structure," "Agglomeration Economies and the C.B.D.," "Urban Growth," "City Size and Distribution," "Urban Ideologies," "Planning Problems," "The Urban Public Economy," "Transportation," "Crime," "Poverty," "Unemployment," "Economics of the Ghetto," "Housing," and "Environmental Problems and Policy."

Schreiber, Arthur F.; Gatons, Paul K.; and Clemmer, Richard B. ECONOMICS OF URBAN PROBLEMS: AN INTRODUCTION. 2d ed. New York: Houghton Mifflin, 1976. xiii, 402 p. Index, pp. 398-402.

> This text presents students with some fundamental tools in economics and then applies them to urban problems. No background in economics is required. Review and discussion questions and suggested readings conclude each chapter. The sixteen chapters cover the following areas: "Land Use and Location," "Economic Efficiency, Analysis of Urban Problems," "Efficiency and Equity," "Poverty," "Urban Housing Problems and Programs," "Urban Transportation,"

"Pollution," "Crime," "The Public Sector," and "Benefits and
Costs of Urbanization." The authors have also published a book
of readings which may be used with this or other texts which are
cited below.

_____. ECONOMICS OF URBAN PROBLEMS: SELECTED READINGS. New
York: Houghton Mifflin, 1971. 278 p. No index.

Segal, David. URBAN ECONOMICS. Homewood, Ill.: Richard D. Irvin,
1977. xiii, 322 p. Index, pp. 315-22.

This text assumes the student has a familiarity with microeconomics
and applies micro-principles to a wide range of issues. Spatial
and locational aspects are discussed early in this text as is urban
size. The examination then proceeds to the economy of the city,
land use, housing, and transportation. Three chapters are devoted
to the separate black-and-white economies and the ghetto. The
book concludes with a discussion of urban public finance. A
variety of appendixes deal with the more "formal" aspects of the
subject matter.

*Smith, Robert H.; Taffee, Edward J.; and King, Leslie J., eds. READINGS
IN ECONOMIC GEOGRAPHY: THE LOCATION OF ECONOMIC ACTIVITY.
Chicago: Rand McNally and Co., 1968. 406 p. Index, pp. 401-06.

*Tabb, William K., and Sawers, Larry, eds. MARXISM AND THE METROP-
OLIS: NEW PERSPECTIVES IN URBAN POLITICAL ECONOMY. New York:
Oxford University Press, 1978. viii, 376 p. Index pp, 368-76.

Thompson, Wilbur. A PREFACE TO URBAN ECONOMICS. Baltimore: Johns
Hopkins Press for Resources for the Future, 1965. xiii, 413 p. Index, pp.
385-413.

In this, the grandfather of all urban economics texts, Thompson
has designed a course which requires principles of economics.
While many parts have been redone in other books, some sections
still remain as classics in the way ideas are shared and thought
is stimulated about the urban economic issues. Part I deals with
the "Principles: Goals and Processes in the Urban Economy" and
includes chapters on: "Economic Growth and Development: Processes, Stages and Determinants," "Money Income and Real Income:
From Labor Markets to Urban Efficiency," "Income Inequality: Personal and Government Poverty," and "Patterns of Economic Insta-
bility: Preventatives and Cures," "Interactions Among Goals:
Opportunity Cost at the Policy Level." Part II, "Prescription:
Problems and Policy in the Urban Economy," discusses: "Urban
Poverty: Employment, Employability and Welfare," "The Urban
Public Economy: Problems in Scale and Choice," "Housing and
Land Use Patterns: Renewal, Race and Sprawl," "Traffic Con-

gestion: Price Rationing and Capital Planning," and "Interactions among Problems: The Problems of "Solutions."

*Venetoulis, Theodore G., and Eisenhauer, Ward, eds. UP AGAINST THE URBAN WALL. Englewood Cliffs, N.J.: Prenctice-Hall, 1971. v, 546 p. Index, pp. 543-46.

*Wilson, James Q., ed. THE METROPOLITAN ENIGMA. Garden City, N.J.: Doubleday and Co., 1968. x, 392 p. Index, pp. 377-92.

Winger, Alan R. URBAN ECONOMICS: AN INTRODUCTION. Columbus: Charles E. Merrill Publishing Co., 1977. viii, 374 p. Index, pp. 367-74.

This text provides an application approach to urban economic problems by first dealing with economic theory to give unity and a foundation for the more detailed examination of urban problems. "The Theory" is presented in part I and deals with scale economies, transportation costs, location and central place theory, macro models of urban growth, (both demand and supply), city structure, urban real estate markets, and the performance of the urban economy in terms of equity and cost-benefit analyses. Part II presents material on urban history, urbanization, and the future. "Problems of Urban Areas" is the topic of part III. Specific attention is given to poverty, housing, transportation, the public economy, and city size. Part IV discusses urban planning, and part V is concerned with various models of urban growth such as economic base, input-output, economic forecasting, and urban simulation models.

Chapter 9
URBAN BIBLIOGRAPHIES

Black, Alan. URBAN DENSITY PROFILES: A GUIDE TO THE LITERATURE. Monticello, Ill.: Council of Planning Librarians, 1976. 41 p. Bibliography, pp. 28-40.

This is a simple discussion of population research and mathematical models in conjunction with urban economics. One also finds a discussion of urban density and a review of that literature.

Brunn, Stanley D. URBANIZATION IN DEVELOPING COUNTRIES: AN INTERNATIONAL BIBLIOGRAPHY. East Lansing: Latin American Studies Center, Michigan State University, 1971. xviii, 693 p. Index, pp. 683-93.

This is an interdisciplinary, multilingual bibliography of the patterns, processes, and problems of cities in the developing world. It contains 7,138 entries.

Fritschler, A. Lee; Harman, B. Douglas; and Ross, Bernard H. URBAN AFFAIRS BIBLIOGRAPHY: A GUIDE TO THE LITERATURE IN THE FIELD. Washington, D.C.: School of Government and Public Administration, American University, 1970. iv, 94 p. No index.

This is for students of urban affairs; it is a highly selected group of references. The bias is to politics, and three pages are devoted to references in urban economics. It is not annotated.

Hoover, Dwight W. CITIES. New York: R.R. Bowker Co., 1976. x, 231 p. Author Index, pp. 203-10. Title Index, pp. 211-31.

The two parts of this bibliography are the city in practice and the city in perspective. Traditional problems in urban economics are listed in the first part, including blacks, housing, education, transportation, urban and suburban studies, crime, civic disorders, urban poverty and urban reform. Part II contains listings of perspectives of urban theory, images, planning, sociology, geography, history, economics, and government. Included is a list of "Journals of Urban Themes."

Hudson, Barbara, and McDonald, Robert H. METROPOLITAN COMMUNITIES: A BIBLIOGRAPHY WITH SPECIAL EMPHASIS UPON GOVERNMENT AND POLITICS 1908-70. Chicago: Public Administration Service, 1972.

> This listing of works concerning metropolitan areas in the United States deals mostly with studies relating to the political and governmental aspects of cities. Some works in economics are cited.

Keys, Scott. URBAN AND REGIONAL STUDIES AT U.S. UNIVERSITIES. Baltimore: Johns Hopkins Press for Resources for the Future, 1964. viii, 127 p. Index of Agencies, pp. 107-21. Index of Persons, pp. 122-27.

> This report is based on a 1963 study of urban and regional research. Both publications and work in progress is included in this review of some 700 studies. Topic areas range from historical trends, economics, and demography to land use and government.

Nijhoff, Martenies. METROPOLIS: A SELECT BIBLIOGRAPHY OF METROPOLITAN AREAS. The Hague: Mouton, 1967. xiii, 265 p.

> This is an international listing which includes 28 countries, covers topics in administration and organization, health, finance, education, housing, planning, and other urban problems. A section on economics is included as well. U.S. and Canadian sources were omitted. There are 267 entries.

Travis, Irene; Burbank, Judith; and Rothchild, Joan. TECHNOLOGY AND THE CITY. Research Review, no. 5. Cambridge, Mass.: Harvard University, Program in Technology and Society, 1970. v, 55 p.

> This report reviews the relevant literature, abstracting from books and articles, and assessing their impact on the field. Areas of interest to urban economists include: technology and urban form, transportation, planning, and new towns.

U.S. Congress. Senate. Committee on Government Operations. METROPOLITAN AMERICA: A SELECTED BIBLIOGRAPHY. 88th Cong., 2d sess. Washington, D.C.: Government Printing Office, 1964. v, 37 p. Author Index, pp. 35-37.

> This is a topically arranged and annotated bibliography of the "more significant" books and reports in the field.

Part II

REGIONAL ECONOMICS

Chapter 10

REGIONAL ECONOMICS: GENERAL APPROACHES

Bendavid-Val, Avrom. REGIONAL ECONOMIC ANALYSIS FOR PRACTITIO-
NERS: AN INTRODUCTION TO COMMON DESCRIPTIVE METHODS. Rev. ed.
New York: Praeger, 1974. xx, 202 p. Bibliography, pp. 179–202.

This book is an outgrowth of a course in regional development
planning for noneconomists, and it contains little in the way of
theory or models. It is a "simplified means of performing the
more common and most widely useful descriptive methods of regional development." Topics which are covered are: "An Introduction to Regional Thinking," "The Basic Regional, Statistical
Compendium," "Income Measures, Regional and Social Accounting,"
"Linkages, Flows and Regional Balance of Payments Studies," "Relative Regional Industrial Composition Analysis," "Economic Base
Analysis," and "Regional Input-Output Analysis." "Learning Exercises" are found at the end of each chapter.

Bergsman, Joel; Greenston, Peter; and Healy, Robert. THE AGGLOMERATION
PROCESS. Washington, D.C.: Urban Institute, 1973. 26 p.

This is a classification of economic activities based on location
patterns.

Brewis, T.N. REGIONAL ECONOMIC POLICIES IN CANADA. Toronto:
Macmillan Co., 1969. 303 p. Suggested Readings, pp. 283–88. Index, pp.
289–303. Figures and tables.

This is a review of the Canadian experience in the realm of spatial
economics. Its purpose is to examine issues and area development
policies as they affect the Canadian scene. Specific chapters
deal with: "Spatial Characteristics of the Economy," "Industrial
Location and its Determinants," "The Demarcation of Regions,"
"The Assessment and Determinants of Regional Growth," "The
Grounds for Regional Development Policies, Underemployment and
Unemployment," and "Rural Poverty, the Agriculture and Rural
Development Programs." The role of the provincial governments
is considered, and changes are recommended in Canadian regional
planning.

Brown, A.J. THE FRAMEWORK OF REGIONAL ECONOMICS IN THE UNITED KINGDOM. Cambridge, Engl.: University Press, 1972. xviii, 370 p. Index. Tables and charts.

This book deals with the policy and theory of regional economics. It is comprehensive in its scope, examining real income differentials, regional growth, population change, the structure of growth, optional size, growth dynamics, regional capital movements, factor movements, and policy.

Brown, A.J., and Burrows, E.M. REGIONAL ECONOMIC PROBLEMS: COMPARATIVE EXPERIENCES OF SOME MARKET ECONOMIES. London: Allen and Unwin, 1977. 209 p. References and Further Reading, pp. 200-206. Index, pp. 206-9.

This is a discussion about how regional problems arose and what might be done about them and how policies might be developed to allow a region to cope with these problems. Policies used in the United States, the United Kingdom, and Western Europe are compared with a focus on four broad kinds of problem regions: agricultural regions, coal mining regions, old textile regions, and congested regions. This is not a book of techniques.

Foust, J. Brady, and deSouza, Anthony R. ECONOMIC LANDSCAPE: A THEORETICAL INTRODUCTION. Columbus, Ohio: Charles E. Merrill Publishing Co., 1978. 288 p. Index.

The location of economic activity is the primary consideration of this text. Topic headings are: "Static Models of Optimum Location Patterns" and "Non-Optional Decision-Making and Evolutionary Systems." The economic landscape is then discussed in the context of these two headings with looks at agriculture, retailing and services, manufacturing, transportation, decision-making, and development.

Ghali, M., and Renaud, B. THE STRUCTURE AND DYNAMIC PROPERTIES OF A REGIONAL ECONOMY. Lexington, Mass.: Lexington Books, 1975. xv, 158 p. Appendix: The Data, pp. 141-48. References, pp. 149-54. Index, pp. 155-58.

This book is an account of a long-term project studying regional growth. A large-scale econometric model for Hawaii is developed which portrays the structure of a regional economy during a period of rapid growth.

Hansen, Niles M. THE FUTURE OF NONMETROPOLITAN AMERICA. Lexington, Mass.: Lexington Books, 1973. 256 p. Bibliography, notes, figures, and tables. No index.

This study examines the nonmetropolitan regions which grew in population during the 1960s after previous decline. It examines,

in a national context, the reasons for the turnaround. Chapters
detail "Factors Determining the Location of Economic Activity in
Metropolitan and Nonmetropolitan Areas," "The Role of Highways,"
and "Changes in Employment Structure." The next several chapters
examine particular cases in Minnesota, Wisconsin, the Ozarks, the
Tennessee Valley, Colorado, New Mexico, Vermont, New Hamp-
shire, Northern Georgia, and Central Texas. The study concludes
with a discussion of "Migration and Income Changes in Turnaround
Countries."

Holland, Stuart. CAPITAL VERSUS THE REGIONS. New York: St. Martin's
Press, 1976. vi, 328 p. Tables, pp. 277-87. Figures, pp. 288-300. References, pp. 301-21. Index, pp. 322-28.

Holland argues that current economic theory is inadequate in its
attempts to explain the regional imbalances in the Western capitalist economies. He argues that a new kind of regional planning
is needed to correct the regional inequalities. The eight chapters
deal with: "Theories of Regional Self-Balance," "Theories of
Regional Imbalance," "Imbalanced Growth and Trade," "Migration
and Imbalanced Resource Use," "Unequal Competition and Regional
Imbalance," "Structure Versus the Regions," "Spatial Concentration
Versus Dispersion," and "Theory, Practice and Policy Imperfections."

_____. THE REGIONAL PROBLEM. New York: St. Martin's Press, 1977.
180 p.

The major arguments developed in CAPITAL VERSUS THE REGIONS
are elaborated upon here and applied to regional problems and
policies in the United States and Western Europe. Holland argues
that capitalist regional theory and policies do not take the unequal competition between big and small firms into account. He
further develops the idea of the "meso-economic" sector which
has arisen between the macro- and micro-economic sectors of the
economy. The contents include chapters on "Politics, Economics
and Regions," "Capitalism and Regional Imbalance," "The Limits
of Liberal Capitalists Policies," "The Region in International Integration," "Regions versus Europe," "Federalism and the Regional
Problem," "Strategy for Regional Development," and "Beyond State
Capitalism."

Hoover, Edgar M. AN INTRODUCTION TO REGIONAL ECONOMICS. 2d ed.
New York: Alfred A. Knopf, 1975. xvii, 395 p. Index, pp. 389-95.

This book was designed for use in first courses in regional economics,
and only a minimum background in economics is needed. Topics
covered in the thirteen chapters of the text include: "Individual
Location Decisions," "Transfer Costs," "Location Patterns," "Land
Use," "Towns, Cities, and Regions," "The Location of People,"
"Regional Economic Structure and Growth," "Regional Objectives

and Policies," "The Spatial Structure of Urban Areas," "Changes in Urban Patterns," and "Some Spatial Aspects of Urban Economic Problems."

Isard, Walter. INTRODUCTION TO REGIONAL SCIENCE. Englewood Cliffs, N.J.: Prentice-Hall, 1975. xxii, 506 p. Index, pp. 446-506. Tables and figures.

This text is designed for use in a one-semester course on the subject or in economics, urban studies, or geography. This is a comprehensive account of areas of interest in regional science. Tools are developed from scratch, and they are integrated into a much higher level of discussion and analysis.

Isard, Walter; Bramhall, David F.; Carrothers, Gerald A.P.; Cumberland, John H.; Moses, Leon N.; Pire, Daniel O.; and Schooler, Eugene W. METHODS OF REGIONAL ANALYSIS: AN INTRODUCTION TO REGIONAL SCIENCE. Cambridge: M.I.T. Press, 1960. xxix, 813 p. Index, pp. 784-813.

This is no less than a treatise on most topics that are techniques of concern to the regional scientist. These include population projections, regional income estimation, capital flows, location theory, I-0, L.P., gravity models, and other techniques relevant to regional studies.

Richardson, Harry W. ELEMENTS OF REGIONAL ECONOMICS. Baltimore: Penquin Books, 1969. 166 p. References, pp. 153-60. Index, pp. 161-66.

Richardson has written an extremely brief introduction to regional economics with particular emphasis on space and distance. Regional growth models are examined empirically, and there are occasional methodology discussions concerning empirical analysis. Chapters include discussions on "Regional Income," "Regional Growth," "Location and Agglomeration," "The Nodal Hierarchy," "Problems in Regional Planning," "The Direction of Regional Policy," "Some Regional Planning Techniques," and "Conclusions."

_____. REGIONAL ECONOMICS, LOCATION THEORY, URBAN STRUCTURE, AND REGIONAL CHANGE. New York: Praeger, 1969. xii, 457 p. Paper. Bibliography, pp. 429-42. Name Index, pp. 443-46. Subject Index, pp. 447-57.

This is a comprehensive text which covers the main elements of location and urban and regional economics. Not only are models presented, they are analyzed and critically examined, and suggestions are made as to how they might become more operational. In areas where theory is shallow, Richardson outlines a process along which relevant theories might be developed. In Part A, Location, the analysis first proceeds to "Spatial Price Theory." Next, "Transport Costs and Location" are examined, followed by

"The Optimal Location of the Firm." Part A concludes with the development of "The General Theory of Location." The urban economy is the topic of Part B, and chapters discuss "Urban Spatial Structure," "Urban Growth," and "The Urban Public Economy." The remaining half of the book is devoted to an examination of regional economics, Part C. Here one finds chapters on "The Regional Framework," "Inter-Regional Income Theory," "Regional Business Cycles," "Factor Mobility," "Regional Growth," "Policy Objectives and Efficiency," and "The Strategy of Regional Policy." Mathematics is kept to a minimum, but a knowledge of elementary economics is helpful.

_____. REGIONAL GROWTH THEORY. New York: John Wiley and Sons, 1973. viii, 264 p. References, pp. 237-54. Index of Names, pp. 255-57. Index of Subjects, pp. 258-64.

A theory of regional growth is developed that attempts to integrate space and distance into the analysis of regional growth. The introductory chapter states the problems of regional growth and defines regions. "The Current State of Regional Growth Theory" in chapter 2 outlines export base, neoclassical, input-output, and econometric elements in theory. Chapter 3, "Space and Regional Growth Analysis," reviews location theory, transportation, regional growth, gravity model and growth pole literature. "Resource Mobility in the Space Economy" examines interregional migration and capital mobility. Urban and regional economics are integrated in "Towards a Growth Theory of Spatial Development." Chapter 6 deals with investment, and chapters 7 through 9 set up spatial growth theory, the model, and the policy implications of the theory.

Seibert, Horst. REGIONAL ECONOMIC GROWTH: THEORY AND POLICY. Scranton, Pa.: International Textbook Co., 1969. viii, 217 p. Selected Bibliography, pp. 203-06. Index, pp. 205-17.

In this book, the spatial dimensions of growth theory are developed, first in terms of a closed region and then an open region. Part III presents a formal model using both internal and external growth determinants. There is no empirical verification attempted. Problems are included at the end of each chapter. Students should have a strong calculus background.

Smith, Milo, and Associates. REGIONAL ECONOMIC ANALYSIS: PENSA-COLA SMSA. Pensacola, Fla.: Escambra-Santa Rosa Regional Planning Council, 1973. v, 190 p.

This is an example of an urban development design and plan.

U.S. Department of Commerce. Economic Development Administration. REGIONAL DEVELOPMENT IN THE UNITED STATES. Washington, D.C.: Government Printing Office, 1967.

This volume consists of a series of working papers designed to explain regional development problems and policies in the United
States. Major topic areas include: "The U.S. Economy-An Overview," Administration of Federal Programs," "An Overview of
Regional Planning and Development Policy," "Public Works and
the Economic Development Act of 1965," "Planning Programs for
Economic Development," "Economic Development Regions--Case
Histories," and "Urban Development--Key to Future Regional Economic Development Programs."

Valette, Jean Paul; Kraft, Gerald; and Meyer, John R. THE ROLE OF TRANS-
PORTATION IN REGIONAL ECONOMIC DEVELOPMENT. Lexington, Mass.:
Lexington Books, 1971. 112 p. Bibliography, pp. 109-12.

This book takes issue with the theory that investment in transportation will induce regional growth. The analysis deals with the
United States, where the transportation system is well developed,
and where industry is relocating and locating only partially for
transportation networks.

Whitby, M.C.; Tansey, A.W.; Roblins, D.L.J.; and Willis, K.G. RURAL
RESOURCE DEVELOPMENT. London: Methuen, 1974. 240 p.

This is a text dealing with the problems of predicting and explaining economic variables and with the various institutions and groups
that influence rural policy. It is an interdisciplinary approach
designed for planners, agricultural economists, and rural geographers.

Chapter 11
REGIONAL GROWTH AND DEVELOPMENT

Alonso, William. INDUSTRIAL LOCATION AND REGIONAL POLICY IN ECONOMIC DEVELOPMENT. Berkeley: Institute of Urban and Regional Development, University of California, 1963.

Ashby, L.D. GROWTH PATTERNS IN EMPLOYMENT BY COUNTY, 1940-1950 AND 1950-1960. 8 vols. Washington, D.C.: Government Printing Office, 1965.

Barkin, David, and King, Timothy. REGIONAL ECONOMIC DEVELOPMENT: THE RIVER BASIN APPROACH IN MEXICO. Cambridge: Cambridge University Press, 1970. x, 262 p. Index, 257-62. Maps. Bibliographical references at the end of each chapter.

> This book offers coverage of the Tepaleatepec Commission and the development of the river basin. The first part examines governmental policies designed to solve regional economic development problems in LDCs, and the second part is devoted to an examination of the river basin approach in Mexico. Though it is written primarily for economists, others can understand and utilize the work with some omissions.

Bernard, Philippe. GROWTH POLES AND GROWTH CENTERS IN REGIONAL DEVELOPMENT. 3 vols. Geneva: United Nations Research Institute for Social Development, 1970.

Bolton, R.E. DEFENSE PURCHASES AND REGIONAL GROWTH. Washington, D.C.: Brookings Institution, 1966. xiv, 189 p. Appendix, pp. 151-74. Bibliography, pp. 175-80. Index, pp. 181-89.

> A simple model of regional growth is developed which estimates the contribution of defense income between 1952 and 1962 by state and region. A description of the procedures used is given, as is some of the data. The main analysis discusses the rate of growth of personal income provided by the rate of growth of exogeneous income. Nine census regions were used in the analysis.

Cameron, G.C. REGIONAL ECONOMIC DEVELOPMENT: THE FEDERAL ROLE. Baltimore: Johns Hopkins Press, 1970. ix, 161 p. Appendix: Public Works and Economic Development Act of 1965.

This monograph discusses federal involvement with area and regional redevelopment. The chapters examine "The Case for Federal Involvement," "Growth Centers and the Areas of Severe Distress," "The Evolving Federal Role--The Legislated Framework," "The Evolving Federal Strategy--Program Implementation," and "National, Regional, and State Planning and the Regional Action Planning Commissions."

Chisholm, Michael. THE FUTURE OF THE CITY REGION. Glasgow: Social Science Research Council, Center for Environmental Studies, 1968.

This paper is a report of the more important issues which arose from papers presented at a conference of the SSRC/CES held at Glasgow University in 1968. The discussions of these papers is also reported. The theme of the papers concerns what city regions will be like in the future.

Conference on Research in Income and Wealth. REGIONAL INCOME. Vol. 21. Princeton, N.J.: Princeton University Press, 1957. x, 408 p. Author Index, pp. 401-02. Subject Index, pp. 401-08.

Conroy, Michael E. REGIONAL ECONOMIC GROWTH, DIVERSIFICATION AND CONTROL. New York: Praeger, 1975. xv, 163 p. Appendixes, pp. 119-51. References, pp. 152-57. Index, pp. 158-63.

The central focus of this study is an "analysis of the industrial structure of regions under uncertainty conditions." A model is developed "which is used to demonstrate that in most cases a diversified industrial structure will be the most efficient form of trading-off the risks and returns of alternative industrial structures."

Cumberland, John H. REGIONAL DEVELOPMENT EXPERIENCES AND PROSPECTS IN THE UNITED STATES OF AMERICA. The Hague: Mouton, 1971. xvi, 170 p. Statistical sources, pp. 147-62. Research Needs, pp. 163-64. Bibliography and References, pp. 165-70. Figures and Tables.

This is one of a series of reports of research sponsored by the U.N. Research Institute for Social Development. A major account of regional economic development in the United States is provided, including discussions of the infrastructure, river basin development, ARA, EDA, ARC, and other regional commissions. The future of regional development in the United States is also discussed.

Darwent, David F. GROWTH POLE AND CENTER CONCEPTS: A REVIEW, EVALUATION AND BIBLIOGRAPHY. Working Paper. Berkeley: Institute of Urban and Regional Development, University of California, 1968. 49 p.

This is a review, discussion, and critique of the growth center literature to date. The selected bibliography contains 149 French and U.S. listings.

Denoon, David, and Meyer, John R. TECHNOLOGICAL CHANGE, MIGRATION PATTERNS, AND SOME ISSUES OF PUBLIC POLICY. Cambridge: Harvard University Press, 1967. 21 p. Bibliography.

Part of a program on regional and urban economics, this discussion paper deals with the effects that innovations and changes in techniques have on migration. Policy suggestions are also made.

Friedman, John. REGIONAL DEVELOPMENT POLICY: A CASE STUDY OF VENEZUELA. Cambridge: M.I.T. Press, 1966. 279 p. Index, pp. 273-79.

In the first part, spatial elements are incorporated into economic development processes, and the second part of the book is devoted to a case study of regional development policy in Venezuela. Part I involves an examination of the "Structure and Process of Regional Development," with discussions centering on the problems, goals, and approaches to regional development. The case study which is the focus of part II centers on urbanization, and the elements and the problems of a regional policy.

Fullerton, Herbert H., and Prescott, James R. AN ECONOMIC SIMULATION MODEL FOR REGIONAL DEVELOPMENT PLANNING. Ann Arbor, Mich.: Ann Arbor Science Publishers, 1975. viii, 133 p. References, pp. 125-28. Index, pp. 129-33.

This is a presentation of a model which was developed to aid regional planning in the state of Iowa. The model consists of some ninety equations and includes six sectors. There is a general discussion of models and their application as well.

Green, G. COMMUNITY SIZE AND AGGLOMERATION OF TRADE, SERVICE AND OTHER LOCALLY ORIENTED INDUSTRIES. St. Louis: Institute of Urban and Regional Studies, Washington University, 1966. ii, 31 p. No index.

This report is part of a study of the impact of water resource investment projects on a region. Green tests the assumption that employment in locally serving activities rises more than in proportion to the growth in total employment.

Green, James L. METROPOLITAN ECONOMIC REPUBLICS: A CASE STUDY IN REGIONAL ECONOMIC GROWTH. Athens: University of Georgia Press, 1965. x, 206 p. Index.

This is a look at Atlanta as a model for community action in maintaining high levels of employment and income stability. The metropolitan-regional model examines Atlanta as a regional center in a Keynesian macro framework. An input-output analysis is also utilized.

Hale, Carl. THE CONTRIBUTION OF LOCAL SUBSIDIES IN THE ECONOMIC DEVELOPMENT OF WEST VIRGINIA. Economic Development Series, no. 12. Morgantown, W. Va.: Bureau of Business Research, College of Commerce and Office of Research and Development, Center for Appalachian Studies and Development, 1969. v, 56 p.

This report, covering the period 1956-67, discusses the kinds of subsidies involved, the location factors involved, and a method for evaluating industry subsidy actions. Findings from the quantitative study indicate that these activities cause the spread of intraregional investment.

Hansen, Niles M. GROWTH CENTERS AND REGIONAL DEVELOPMENT: SOME PRELIMINARY CONSIDERATIONS. Discussion Paper, no. 5. Lexington, Ky.: Center for Developmental Change, 1968. 48 p. Selected Bibliography of Growth, pp. 46-48.

This is an examination of different types of regions and a review of growth center strategies for these areas. Other discussion papers in this series include:

APPRENTICESHIP AND ON-THE-JOB TRAINING PROGRAMS IN SOUTHERN GROWTH CENTERS, by Richard Snarr.
DUALISM AND GROWTH POTENTIAL, by Richard Gift.
AN EVALUATION OF LOCAL INDUSTRIAL SUBSIDIES FOR REGIONAL DEVELOPMENT, by John D. Milliken.
FACTOR MIGRATION: TRADE THEORY AND GROWTH CENTERS, by Charles W. Hultman.
GROWTH CENTER POLICY IN THE UNITED STATES, by Niles M. Hansen.
GROWTH CENTER STRATEGY FOR SOUTH TEXAS, by Michael Curley.
A GROWTH CENTER STRATEGY FOR THE UNITED STATES, by Niles M. Hansen.
HOUSING THE LOW INCOME MIGRANT: AN ISSUE IN HOUSING DEVELOPMENT, by Alan Winger and Gary Mammel.
LABOR MOBILITY AND REGIONAL PAYMENTS ADJUSTMENTS, by Charles W. Hultman.
MONETARY VARIABLES AND REGIONAL ECONOMIC GROWTH, by Alan Winger.
ON THRESHOLDS, TAKE-OFFS AND SPURTS: A PLACE FOR SMSA'S IN GROWTH CENTER STRATEGY, by Jean Shackelford.
THE OZARKS REGION: A GROWTH CENTER STRATEGY, by Eldon J. Nosari.
A PRELIMINARY EVALUATION OF LEXINGTON, KENTUCKY AS A GROWTH CENTER FOR THE PEOPLE OF EASTERN KENTUCKY, by Niles M. Hansen.
RECENT DEVELOPMENTS IN FRENCH REGIONAL PLANNING AND THEIR SIGNIFICANCE FOR AMERICAN REGIONAL POLICY, by Niles Hansen.
A REGIONAL ECONOMIC GROWTH MODEL, by Alan Winger.

REGIONAL ECONOMICS AND THE NEW REGIONALISM, by
Niles M. Hansen.
URBAN ALTERNATIVES TO RURAL POVERTY, by Niles M. Hansen.
URBAN PROBLEMS AND ECONOMIC THEORY, by Alan Winger
and John Madden.

Henderson, James Michael, and Krueger, Anne O. NATIONAL GROWTH
AND ECONOMIC CHANGE IN THE MIDWEST. Minneapolis: University of
Minnesota Press, 1965. xiii, 231 p. Index, pp. 229-31. Tables and figures.

This publication of the Upper Midwest Economic Study provides an
analysis of the structure and growth of the area between 1950 and
1975, policies, and a discussion of the various sectors during this
period. Appendixes cover methodology, economic base and data
projections, county indicators, data maintenance, and the like.

Hermansen, Iormod. INTERREGIONAL ALLOCATION AND INVESTMENTS
FOR SOCIAL AND ECONOMIC DEVELOPMENT. U.N. Research Institute
for Social Development, report no. 70.4. Geneva: 1970. iv, 61 p.

This is a report-monograph stressing the use of investment funds in
regions of developing countries. Two types of simplified two-region
growth models are set forth: one with fixed structural parameters,
the other with built in changes in the parameters.

Hewings, Geoffrey J.D. REGIONAL INDUSTRIAL ANALYSIS AND DEVELOP-
MENT. New York: St. Martin's Press, 1977. 180 p. References, pp. 158-
70. Appendix: Guide to Major Journals Publishing Articles in the Area of
Regional Industrial Analysis, pp. 171-73. Author Index, pp. 174-77. Subject
Index, pp. 177-80.

Some of the "more important techniques of regional analysis" are
examined in this work. These techniques are derived from geography, regional economics, and regional science. Chapters include: "Underlying Need for Regional Analysis and Development,"
"Economic Base and Trade Flows Analysis," "Regional and Interregional Structure: Interindustry Models," "Theories of Regional
Economic Growth and Development," and "Implementation of Development: Public Policy Issues."

Hilhorst, J.G.M. REGIONAL DEVELOPMENT THEORY: AN ATTEMPT TO
SYNTHESIZE. The Hague: Mouton, 1967. 37 p. References, pp. 36-37.

This reprint of a lecture deals with the failure of economists,
geographers, planners, and sociologists to successfully present a
regional development theory, and the major difficulties in doing
so. Hilhorst then reviews the major contributions to the development of regions and discusses the elements which he believes
should underlie some sort of synthesis.

Krutilla, John V., and Eckstein, Otto. MULTIPLE PURPOSE RIVER DEVELOP-
MENT: STUDIES IN APPLIED ECONOMIC ANALYSIS. Baltimore: Johns
Hopkins Press for Resources for the Future, 1958. 316 p. Paper.

A framework is put forth for analyzing the economic efficiency of
particular river basin programs.

Leven, Charles L.; Legler, J.B.; and Shapiro, P. AN ANALYTICAL FRAME-
WORK FOR REGIONAL DEVELOPMENT POLICY. Cambridge: M.I.T. Press,
1970. 193 p. References, pp. 178-86. Index, pp. 187-93.

This is an examination of the analytical problems of developing
a systematic set of social accounts for a system of regions where
this added regional feature can be incorporated into a national
economic development policy. Shortcomings of national income
and product accounts are avoided, and regional parochial interests
are put aside so that a clear "set of principles for construction of
a multiregional system of accounts and data for determination of
policy at federal, state, and local levels emerges."

Lynch, John E. LOCAL ECONOMIC DEVELOPMENT AFTER MILITARY BASE
CLOSURES. New York: Praeger, 1970. xxiv, 350 p. Index, p. 274.

Many cases are examined in this book on the effects of some 950
cutbacks between 1961 and 1969. The effects on the various
sectors of the local economy are examined, and forecasts are made
for the future of urban areas which experience either a cutback in
military expenditures in the area or a withdrawal of a military base.
Data is included.

McCrone, Gavin. REGIONAL POLICY IN BRITAIN. 5th ed. London:
George Allen and Unwin, 1976. 280 p. Index, pp. 278-80.

Regional policy in the United Kingdom changed during the 1940s
and 50s in response to Keynesian economics. This work views
the development of that policy and its continued change and revision. An appraisal of British regional policy is offered as well.

Macy, Bruce W.; Bednar, James M.; and Roberts, Robert E. IMPACT OF
SCIENCE AND TECHNOLOGY ON REGIONAL DEVELOPMENT. Prepared by
the Midwest Research Institute for the U.S. Department of Commerce, Economic
Development Administration. Washington, D.C.: Government Printing Office,
December 1967. iv, 168 p.

This is an examination of the ways in which science and technology
are related to the process of regional growth. Included are discussions of the characteristics of science and technology and the
importance of science and technology to the Regional Commissions.

Mera, Kolchi. INCOME DISTRIBUTION AND REGIONAL DEVELOPMENT.

Tokyo: University of Tokyo Press, 1975. xv, 242 p. References, pp. 237-42. No index.

This monograph examines the income distribution issue in a regional development framework using marginal productivity theory. The ten chapters are devoted to discussions of "Urban Agglomerations and Economic Efficiency," "An Equilibrium Model of Regional Growth: The Case of the U.S.," "Regional Production Functions and Social Overhead Capital: The Japanese Case," "The Trade-off Between Aggregate Efficiency and Interregional Equity," "A Dynamic Implication of Static Inefficiency," and "A Dynamic Analysis of Two Regions with Immobile Factors."

Miernyk, William H. THE CHANGING STRUCTURE OF THE SOUTHERN ECONOMY. Research Triangle Park, N.C.: Southern Growth Policies Board, 1977. 44 p. References, pp. 43-4.

This paper was commissioned for a conference on the future of the South's economy and discusses the steady growth-no growth arguments in a regional setting. The economic structure and framework of the area are analyzed, and a future outlook for income and structure is offered.

Oklahoma. State University. Department of Agricultural Economics. REGIONAL ECONOMIC DEVELOPMENT: PROCEEDINGS OF A METHODOLOGY WORKSHOP. Stillwater: 1966. iv, 135 p.

The workshop, held in Denver in May, 1966, was sponsored by the Great Plains Resource Committee. The purpose was to examine methodology in regional economic development and to present new ideas and concepts for future research. Among the topics of the seven papers are an examination of problem areas, goal specification, I-0 analysis, and dynamic growth theory.

Perloff, Harvey S., with Dodds, Vera W. HOW A REGION GROWS: AREA DEVELOPMENT IN THE U.S. ECONOMY. Supplementary Paper, no. 17. New York: Committee for Economic Development, 1963. 147 p. Paper.

This book is basically a condensed version of REGIONS RESOURCES AND ECONOMIC GROWTH that employs more recent statistical data and includes a clarification of the implications of the data. Chapters include: "Changing Patterns of Regional Growth," "Factors Behind the Volume Growth of Regions," "Long Term Changes in Regional Distribution of Economic Activity," "Growth of States in Recent Years," "Recent Shifts in Employment Among the States," "Changes in Mining, Agricultural, and Manufacturing Employment," "Per Capita Income," "Levels and Rates of Growth," and "Approaches to Regional Development."

Perloff, Harvey S.; Dunn, Edgar S., Jr.; Lampard, Eric E.; and Muth, Richard F. REGIONS RESOURCES AND ECONOMIC GROWTH. Baltimore: Johns

Hopkins Press for Resources for the Future, 1960. xxv, 716 p. Paper. Statistical Appendix, pp. 609-84. Index, pp. 685-716.

Ths objective of this study was to view the differences in economic growth in the United States among the various regions. Information is provided for both private and public groups interested in aspects of regional growth, and a conceptual and methodological framework is given as a guide for future research. Economic growth over space and time is examined. The five major sections of the book are devoted to: "An Historical Review of Regional Economic Growth," "A Framework for Analysis," "Regional Economic Development 1870-1950," "The Regional Distribution of Economic Activity in the U.S., 1939-1954," and "Variations in Levels and Rates of Growth of Per Capita Income."

Pred, Alan. THE INTERURBAN TRANSMISSION OF GROWTH IN ADVANCED ECONOMIES. Luxemburg: International Institute of Applied Systems Analysis, 1976.

Romans, J.T. CAPITAL EXPORTS AND GROWTH AMONG U.S. REGIONS. Middletown, Ohio: Wesleyan University Press, 1965. xv, 236 p. 11 Appendix Tables, pp. 150-223. Selected Bibliography, and Major Sources of Data, pp. 225-30. No index.

This book serves two main purposes: (1) "to present heretofore unavailable estimates of regional income and output and of the transmission of capital between regions," and (2) "to analyze the relationship between regional income, capital movements and growth rates." Interregional capital movements within the United States are then examined according to their direction and their size. A general framework is developed in the first chapter, and the remaining eight chapters examine the measures of regional accounts, income and capital flows, economic growth, and regional export balances.

Sample, C. James. PATTERNS OF REGIONAL ECONOMIC CHANGE: A QUANTITATIVE ANALYSIS OF U.S. REGIONAL GROWTH AND DEVELOPMENT. Cambridge, Mass.: Ballinger Publishing Co., 1974. xix, 296 p. Bibliography, pp. 273-78. Notes, pp. 279-90. Index, pp. 291-96.

Three different measures of economic change are used in this analysis. They are, per capita income, the average annual rate of increase in total personal income, and the average annual rate of increase in per capita income. The premise of Sample's argument is that "because of different histories, traditions and social economic environments, major regions of the United States have undergone different patterns of development." The analysis makes use of and shows the relative importance of export base arguments.

Sant, Morgan E.C. INDUSTRIAL MOVEMENT AND REGIONAL DEVELOP-
MENT: THE BRITISH CASE. Urban and Regional Planning Series, vol. 11.
New York: Pergamon Press, 1975. 268 p. Index.

This is an examination of how industrial movement has effected
regional growth and development in the United Kingdom over the
past quarter century. Both spatial and temporal analyses are integrated into this discussion of industrial movement. Contents include chapters entitled: "Regional Equilibrium," "Political Intervention and Industrial Movement," "Perspectives on Industrial
Movement," "Time Series," "Geographical Distribution," "The
Prospects for Industrial Mobility," "The Impact of Industrial Movement," and "The Future of Regional Policy in Britain."

Saville, Lloyd. REGIONAL DEVELOPMENT IN ITALY. Durham, N.C.:
Duke University Press, 1967. xiv, 191 p. Index, pp. 175-91. Tables.

This book looks at the historical aspects and the scope of the
regional development problem in Italy as well as the components
of production, development, and growth. It takes a developmental
rather than a regional approach.

Chapter 12

REGIONAL PROBLEMS, POLICY, AND PLANNING

A. GENERAL APPROACHES

Allen, K.J., and McLennan, M.C. REGIONAL PROBLEMS AND POLICIES
IN ITALY AND FRANCE. Beverly Hills, Calif.: Sage Publications, 1970.
xvi, 352 p. Index, p. 350.

> The aim of this study is to examine regional problems and policy
> in Western Europe with the view that the promotion of economic
> growth requires changes of economic structures. Three issues in
> policy are examined: regional planning, growth center policy,
> and the E.E.C. and regional policy.

Bonner, E.R., and Fahle, V.L. TECHNIQUES FOR AREA PLANNING. Pittsburgh: Regional Economic Development Institute, 1967.

Borts, George H., and Stein, Jerome L. ECONOMIC GROWTH IN A FREE
MARKET. New York: Columbia University Press, 1964. 235 p. Notes, pp.
217-32. Index, pp. 233-35.

> Research that has been carried out by the authors in the area of
> regional economics is reported in this monograph. Borts and Stein
> first introduce the "Framework for an Analysis of Economic Growth
> Among Open Economies." Next, they examine the "Empirical
> Regularities in the Process of Growth and Decline," and develop
> "A Critique of a Simple Aggregative Theory of Growth." They
> then turn to an analysis of "Interstate Differences in Rates of
> Growth of Manufacturing," "Interindustry Repercussions of Growth
> and Decline," and "Models of Growth and Allocation." Income
> distribution and capital movement is then examined in terms of
> economic growth, as are governmental policies.

Boudeville, J.R. PROBLEMS OF REGIONAL ECONOMIC PLANNING. Edinburgh: University Press, 1966. 192 p. Index, pp. 173-92.

> This is a series of six lectures ranging from French planning and
> economic thought to an examination of tools for regional economic

studies and programs. Three concepts of space are discussed early
in "Concepts and Definitions" and are used in other parts of the
work. Other subjects which are examined include: "The Tools
for Regional Economic Studies," "Regional Economic Programs,"
"Regional Operational Models," "The Fourth French Plan," and
"French Regional Planning."

Chadwick, G.F. A SYSTEMS VIEW OF PLANNING: TOWARDS A THEORY
OF URBAN AND REGIONAL PLANNING PROCESS. Oxford: Pergamon Press,
1971. xiii, 390 p. Notes on Mathematics, p. 376. Glossary, pp. 377-80.
Index, pp. 381-90.

A general method is employed in this work which "sets out to be
a theory of the process of regional planning." The philosophy and
method are those of the author. The work is mathematical in
nature, dealing with planning, systems, space, operational methods,
modelling, evaluation, and the spatial method of regional planning.

Gillie, F.B. BASIC THINKING IN REGIONAL PLANNING. The Hague:
Mouton, 1967. 95 p. No index.

In addition to explaining what planners do, a large section of
this book is spent discussing the economic activities related to
regional planning.

Hansen, Niles M. FRENCH REGIONAL PLANNING. Bloomington: Indiana
University Press, 1968. xvi, 335 p. Index, pp. 319-55.

This is an examination of the comprehensive French regional planning methods and theory using decentralization, lagging regions
policy, public investment, and others. The work then looks at
ways of applying these ideas to the American economy through
institutions such as the Economic Development Administration and
the Appalachian Regional Commission.

Harrison, A.J. ECONOMICS AND LAND USE PLANNING. London: Croom
Helm, 1977. 256 p. Bibliography, pp. 246-53. Index, pp. 254-56.

The purpose of this book is to develop a framework within which
to examine and appraise land use policies by relating land use
planning to economic analysis. While not a part of traditional
urban economics, the techniques of the discipline are used extensively to analyze policy. A microeconomic approach is applied
to policies of land allocation and the control of activities using
land. The principle focus is on the urban land market with suggestions included for intervention by the public sector. The first
part of the book is totally devoted to "Basic Economic Concepts"
(nine chapters) and their use in an urban framework, and to an
examination of the reasons government intervention into urban
land markets might be justifiable. Part 2 examines land use controls and their arrangement to develop a framework for the exami-

nation of intervention. Contents include: "Individuals, Firms, Markets," "Markets in a Spatial Context," "Market Failures," "The Role of the Planning Authority," "Managing Markets," "Land-Use Controls and the Urban Economy," "The Public Sector," "The Private Sector," "The Arrangement of Land Uses," "Evaluation," "Estimating Social Opportunity Costs," "The Measurement of Benefits," and "Alternative Approaches."

Hilhorst, J.G.M. REGIONAL PLANNING: A SYSTEMS APPROACH. Rotterdam: Rotterdam University Press, 1971. xiv, 151 p. No index.

Five propositions--those of Christaller, Lösch, Mydral, Isard and Perroux, and Tinbergan and Friedman are examined in relation to the "Case for Regional Planning," "A Theory of Regional Development," "The Problem of Regionalization," "Regional Development Strategies," and "The Planning Process."

McLoughlin, J.B. URBAN AND REGIONAL PLANNING: A SYSTEMS APPROACH. New York: Praeger, 1969. 331 p. References, pp. 313-24. Index, pp. 325-31.

This book is aimed at providing a framework in which tools from many fields may be integrated in city and regional planning. Both theory and practice are examined and related to a multidisciplinary body (economics, sociology, geography, and political science) of study.

Mennes, J.B.M.; Tinbergen, Jan; and Waardenberg, J. George. THE ELEMENT OF SPACE IN DEVELOPMENT PLANNING. Amsterdam: North Holland Publishing Co., 1969. xiii, 340 p. References, pp. 320-23. Symbols, pp. 324-34. Author Index, pp. 335. Subject Index, pp. 336-40.

This book is devoted to an in-depth account of spatial analysis in a planning context. Both world and national levels are included in this discussion, as are both open and closed economies. Models are surveyed and critiqued, and preparatory studies are outlined. There are six appendixes.

Moseley, Malcolm J. GROWTH CENTRES IN SPATIAL PLANNING. New York: Pergamon Press, 1974. xii, 192 p. Bibliography, pp. 175-88. Index, pp. 189-92.

Moseley begins this work with a review of growth centre theory and growth centre policy. This is followed by an appraisal of the various planning objectives that growth centre policies have been expected to achieve. This work concludes with a group of policy recommendations and a list of research priorities. Chapter headings include: "Growth-Centre Theory and Growth-Centre Policy," "Growth Centres in Practice," "Urban Centres and the Diffusion of Innovations," "Urban Scale and Service Provision," "Agglomeration Economies and the Stimulation of Growth," "Growth Centres: Their Spatial Impact," "The Generation, Interception and Attraction of Migrants," and "Conclusion: Implications for Policy and Research."

The New England Economic Research Foundation. REVIEW OF REGIONAL ECONOMIC RESEARCH AND PLANNING ON NEW ENGLAND: A SURVEY OF EXISTING LITERATURE WITH PARTICULAR REFERENCE TO RESEARCH AND ACTION PLANNING RECOMMENDATIONS. Washington, D.C.: Government Printing Office, 1963 (?). xv, approx. 250 p.

This is a package of information about the Northeast and the economic development and planning projects which have been undertaken.

Richardson, Harry W. REGIONAL POLICY AND PLANNING IN SPAIN. Lexington, Mass.: Lexington Books, 1975. viii, 253 p. Bibliography, pp. 233-44. Names Index, pp. 245-46. Subject Index, pp. 247-53.

This is a normative economic study examining the background of Spanish regional policy in the context of regional development trends. The four three-year plans between 1962 and 1979 are examined, as is the selection of development pole policy.

Rothblatt, Donald N. REGIONAL PLANNING: THE APPALACHIAN EXPERIENCE. Lexington, Mass.: Lexington Books, 1971. 304 p. Notes, tables, figures, maps, appendixes, bibliography, index.

This book examines the establishment of the Appalachian Regional Commission (ARC), analyzes its planning and allocating functions, and evaluates its impact on the region.

B. CASE STUDIES

Aron, Joan B. THE QUEST FOR REGIONAL COOPERATION. Berkeley and Los Angeles: University of California Press, 1969. vi, 255 p. Index, pp. 221-25.

This is mostly a critique of the aborted attempt to create a New York City council of governments which the author hopes will be useful in other areas. Approaches to urban government and its policies are discussed.

Beard, Thomas R., ed. THE LOUISIANA ECONOMY. Baton Rouge, Louisiana State University Press, 1969. vii, 232 p. No Index.

These nine essays deal with issues ranging from the historical development of the Louisiana economy to banking, international trade, public utilities, and revenues in the state.

Berkman, Richard L., and Viscusi, W. Kip. DAMNING THE WEST: RALPH NADER'S STUDY GROUP REPORT ON THE BUREAU OF RECLAMATION. New York: Grossman Publishers, 1973. 272 p.

The reports of both lawyers and economists are included in this publication. At issue are the damage to the environment, agricultural problems, and expenditures of a regional policy.

Borchert, John R., and Adams, Russell B. TRADE CENTERS AND TRADE AREAS OF THE UPPER MIDWEST. Urban Report, no. 3. Minneapolis: University of Minnesota Press, 1963. vi, 47 p. Maps and Tables.

This monograph defines eight categories of trade centers in the region and classifies over 2,000 business communities.

Breese, Gerald, et al. IMPACT OF LARGE INSTALLATIONS ON NEARBY AREAS. Port Hueneme, Calif.: U.S. Naval Civil Engineering Laboratory, 1965. v, 629 p. Bibliography, pp. 616-29.

Part one of this report of the Bureau of Urban Research at Princeton University documents the impact of large industries and government operations at five sites. These are: U.S. Steel in Lower Bucks County, Pennsylvania; Grumman on Long Island; an Air Force Base in Dover, Delaware; Sampson in Seneca County, New York; and the Atomic Energy Area in the Savannah River Area. The second part of the report gives a discussion and analysis of general topics ranging from land use changes, population growth, and the economic base to housing, schools and recreation, and transportation.

Costikyan, Edward N., and Lehman, Maxwell. NEW STRATEGIES FOR REGIONAL COOPERATION: A MODEL FOR THE TRI-STATE NEW YORK-NEW JERSEY-CONNECTICUT AREA. New York: Praeger, 1973. iix, 93 p. Bibliography, pp. 91-93. Maps.

The concept of "functional regions" is stressed throughout this book which makes a recommendation for expanding the New York City jurisdictional area into the surrounding states that share problems of pollution, transportation, water distribution, and solid waste disposal.

Junk, Paul E., et al. PERSONAL INCOME FOR MISSOURI COUNTIES. Columbia: University of Missouri, School of Business and Public Administration, 1968. 277 p. Paper. No index.

This volume has tables showing, by component, the personal income in each of Missouri's 115 counties along with projections and actual figures over the period 1950-1982.

Lynch, John E. LOCAL ECONOMIC DEVELOPMENT AFTER MILITARY BASE CLOSURES. New York: Praeger, 1970. xxiv, 274 p.

This is a data source on aspects of military base withdrawals from urban areas between 1961 and 1969. Individual cases and fore-casts for the future are included.

Newman, Monroe. THE POLITICAL ECONOMY OF APPALACHIA: A CASE STUDY IN REGIONAL INTEGRATION. Lexington, Mass.: Lexington Books, 1972. xviii, 193 p. Notes, pp. 179-88. Index, pp. 189-93. Tables and Figures.

This study examines the Appalachian regional growth experience, looking at policies of the past and the conceptual basis on which to formulate a comprehensive Appalachian program. Development strategies and planning for the area are discussed.

Thomas, George. POVERTY IN THE NONMETROPOLITAN SOUTH: A CASUAL ANALYSIS. Lexington, Mass.: Lexington Books, 1972. 144 p. Notes, Bib-liography.

This is a study which seeks to determine the root of poverty. Five casual theories are examined, and over 800 students were evaluated to trace the impact of each on the existence and continuation of poverty.

Thompson, James H., and Kee, Woo Sik. THE MUNICIPAL REVENUE PROB-LEM IN WEST VIRGINIA. A Report to the Joint Committee on Government and Finance, Sub-Committee on Taxation of the West Virginia Legislature. Morgantown: West Virginia University, Bureau of Business Research, 1968. vii, 61 p. Paper. No index.

This report gives interstate and intrastate comparisons of current municipal revenues, expenditures, and debt and makes suggestions for possible sources of additional revenue for municipalities in the state. Reforms in the current municipal revenue systems are sug-gested.

Chapter 13

LOCATION, LOCATION THEORY, AND SPATIAL ANALYSIS

Beavon, Keith S.O. CENTRAL PLACE THEORY: A REINTERPRETATION. New York: Lingman, 1977. xi, 157 p. References, pp. 144-51. Author Index, pp. 151-52. Subject Index, pp. 153-57.

This book continues in the tradition of Lösch and Christäller and "attempts...to provide the theoretical bases for a continuum of central places at the intra-urban scale." There are two main parts to this book. The first part deals with the early work on central place theory. The second part reexamines the work of Losch and extends it to provide the theoretical approach to central places at the intraurban scale.

Beckman, Martin. LOCATION THEORY. New York: Random House, 1968. xii, 132 p. Author's Index, pp. 127-28. Subject Index, pp. 129-32.

This book was written for intermediate and advanced undergraduates in economics and gives a systematic account of location theory. The approaches of von Thünen and Weber are mixed with discussions of equilibrium and activity analysis. Topics covered include: "The Location of an Economic Activity," "Location of an Industry," "Allocation of Land," "Central Places," "Equilibrium," and "Locational Effects of Economic Growth."

Bos, Hendricus C. SPATIAL DISPERSION OF ECONOMIC ACTIVITY. Rotterdam: Rotterdam University Press, 1965. ix, 100 p. Selected Bibliography, pp. 94-95. List of Symbols, pp. 96-97. Author Index, p. 98. Subject Index, pp. 99-100.

The aim of this work is "to contribute to the understanding of a problem of space economics, the spatial dispersion of economic activity, and to discuss the determination of an optimum spatial dispersion." Chapters are devoted to examining "The Problem," "Earlier Contributions Toward a Theory on Spatial Dispersion," "Dispersion of the Production of One Single Industry," "Several Vertically Integrated Industries," and "Industries Producing Final and Intermediate Products."

Brown, L.A. DIFFUSION PROCESSES AND LOCATION: A CONCEPTUAL FRAMEWORK AND BIBLIOGRAPHY. Philadelphia: Regional Science Research Institute, 1968. vii, 177 p. Subject Index for Bibliographic Entries, pp. 159-68.

Brown presents "guidelines for an attack on the problem of speci-fying a general construct for spatial diffusion research." Discus-sions include "Contributions to a Conceptual Framework of Spatial Diffusion," "Spatial Diffusion Research by Geographers," "Mathe-matical Models," and "Resume and Prospect." A "Bibliography for Spatial Diffusion" concludes the work.

Burrows, James C.; Metcalf, Charles E.; and Kaler, John B. INDUSTRIAL LOCATION IN THE UNITED STATES. Lexington, Mass.: Lexington Books, 1971. 123 p.

Long-run forecasts for economic growth in each of the counties in the United States are made from various socioeconomic data. Mod-els are developed for estimating the future level and mix of an industry. Factors important to these changes are identified and discussed. This is recommended as a reference and for courses in location theory.

Chisholm, Michael. RURAL SETTLEMENT AND LAND USE. Chicago: Aldine, 1970. 207 p. Select Bibliography, pp. 199-202. Index, pp. 203-07.

Distance is considered to be one of the most important factors in location decisions in this work which examines selected features of rural settlement and land use. The contents includes discussions of "Johann Heinrich von Thünen," "More Principles of Location," "The Farm and the Village," "The Region and the World: I," "The Analysis Inverted," "The Farmstead and the Village," "The Region and World: II," and "Technical Change."

Christäller, Walter. CENTRAL PLACES IN SOUTHERN GERMANY. Translated by C.W. Baskin. Englewood Cliffs, N.J.: Prentice-Hall, 1966. 230 p.

This is a classic and original work in central place and location theory. Christäller presents a comprehensive structure of an eco-nomic system which is spatially oriented. He includes political, social, and geographic factors in his systems of hexagonal market nets.

Cotterill, Carl Hayden. INDUSTRIAL PLANT LOCATION: ITS APPLICATION TO ZINC SMELTING. St. Louis: American Zinc, Lead and Smelting Co., 1950. vi, 153 p. Bibliography.

This monograph presents a survey of the zinc smelting industry in the United States in terms of location patterns, techniques employed, location factors, transportation facilities, and logistics. Four case studies apply the techniques of the analysis which is developed in the study.

Czamanski, Stan, with Cyamanski, Daniel Z. STUDY OF SPATIAL INDUSTRIAL COMPLEXES. Halifax, Canada: Institute of Public Affairs, Dalhousie University, 1976. x, 195 p. Bibliography, pp. 93-95. Appendixes, pp. 97-195.

The aim of this monograph is to "verify a broad range of hypotheses dealing with locational preferences of individual plants, clustering and spatial aggregation of industries forming industrial complexes, the impact of industrial location on regional development, and the interrelation between the industrialization and urbanization processes." Part I details a "Study of Clustering of Industries" in examining the problem of statial aggregation. The pull of urban areas, the attraction of firms within industries, size, and types of manufacturing complexes round out the study.

Dacey, Michael. CHRISTALLER'S CENTRAL PLACE STRUCTURES: AN INTRODUCTORY STATEMENT. Northwestern University Studies in Geography, no. 22. Evanston, III.: Northwestern University, Department of Geography, 1977. 311 p.

Estall, R.C., and Buchanan, R. Ogilive. INDUSTRIAL ACTIVITY AND ECONOMIC GEOGRAPHY: A STUDY OF THE FORCES BEHIND THE GEOGRAPHICAL LOCATION OF PRODUCTIVE ACTIVITY IN MANUFACTURING INDUSTRY. London: Hutchinson and Co., 1973. 252 p. Index, pp. 247.

This is a general text giving a "geographical treatment of the economic theorists." A study of the iron and steel industries and the motor vehicle industry provide examples for the discussions on: "Materials, Markets and Transfer Costs in Industrial Location," "Energy Sources and Industrial Location," "The Influence of the Factors of Production," "The Effects of Government Activity," and "Local and Environmental Considerations."

Faden, A.M. THE ECONOMICS OF SPACE AND TIME. Ames: Iowa State University Press, 1977. xiii, 703 p. Title Index, pp. 669-72. Author and Name Index, pp. 673-76. Subject Index, pp. 677-703.

This approach to spatial economics uses the framework of measure theory. It is a comprehensive restructuring of location theory and provides the "Theoretical underpinnings" into which regional economics, regional science, and geography can fit. Chapter 1 details the shortcomings and achievements of the scheme. Chapters 2 and 4 provide an overall descriptive framework. Chapter 3 provides the mathematical model. Chapters 5 and 7 look at the results of the model, and chapter 6 examines markets in general. Chapters 8 and 9 are a reformulation of classical location theory.

Gilmour, James M. SPATIAL EVOLUTION OF MANUFACTURING: SOUTHERN ONTARIO 1851-1891. Toronto: University of Toronto Press, 1972. vxi, 214 p. Index.

An empirical examination of the industrial structure of Ontario is examined in the period 1851-91 to explain the spatial development of manufacturing and changes which occurred in this section. Regional economic growth theory and location theory are the tools used in the analysis.

Greenhut, Melvin L. PLANT LOCATION IN THEORY AND PRACTICE: THE ECONOMIES OF SPACE. Chapel Hill: University of North Carolina Press, 1956. xiii, 338 p. Bibliography, pp. 327-34. Index, pp. 335-38.

Greenhut views "all possible factors in a capitalistic theory of location" in the transition from the purely competitive approaches of the nineteenth and early twentieth century to the monopolistic competition forms of today in seeking some sort of general theory of location. He examines the premise that location of a plant means control over economic areas rather than simply a basis of production operations. Eight case studies are examined using survey and interview data. The major parts of the work are: "Review of Location Theory," "Location Factors," "Empirical Studies," and "A General Theory of Plant Location."

Harris, Curtis C., Jr., and Hopkins, Frank E. LOCATION ANALYSIS: AN INTERREGIONAL ECONOMETRIC MODEL. Lexington, Mass.: Lexington Books, 1972. viv, 316 p. Index, pp. 299-16.

This book presents an interregional, multiindustry model of industrial location. "The model considers two groups of stimuli to industry location--regional factor prices and regional agglomeration effects." Linear programing techniques are used to determine the effect of the transportation industry on location. The work is designed to be the "cornerstone of a larger multiregional, multi-industry forecasting model." Contents include: "The Locational Model," "The Transportation Variables," "Data Requirements," "The Location Equations," and "Location Analysis by Industry."

Hoover, Edgar M. THE LOCATION OF ECONOMIC ACTIVITY. New York: McGraw-Hill, 1948. xv, 310 p. Appendix, pp. 301-2. Select Bibliography, pp. 301-04. Index, pp. 305-10.

Hoover presents the "economics of industrial location, land utilization, urban structure and regional development." Particular attention is paid to the problems of locational change and adjustment with an emphasis on the objective methods and implications of policies of public control. This is an "attempt to bring a more unified and systematic thought to bear on the formulation of principles govering the interrelation of individual locations, the significance of location change, and the scope of public planning and control." The eighteen chapters are broken into four main divisions. These are: "Location Preference and Patterns," "Location Change and Adjustment," "The Locational Significance of Boundaries," and "Locational Objectives and Public Policy."

Isard, Walter. LOCATION AND SPACE-ECONOMY: A GENERAL THEORY RELATING INDUSTRIAL LOCATION, MARKET AREAS, LAND USE, TRADE AND URBAN STRUCTURE. Cambridge: M.I.T. Press, 1956. xix, 350 p. Author Index, p. 289. Subject Index, p. 293. Figures.

> The basic objective of this book is "to improve the spatial and regional framework of the social science discipline--economics-- through the development of a more adequate general theory of location and space-economics." The work is couched in a dy- namic framework to allow an examination of the development process over time. Chapters include discussions of: "Some Gen- eral Theories of Location and Space-Economics," "The Location Equilibrium of the Firm," "Market and Supply Area Analysis and Competitive Location," "Agglomeration Analysis and Agricultural Location Theory," "Some Basic Interrelations of Location and Trade Theory," and "Aspects of General Location Theory: A Mathemati- cal Formulation."

Isard, Walter; Smith, Tony E.; Isard, Peter; Tung, Tze Hsiung; and Dacey, M. GENERAL THEORY: SOCIAL, POLITICAL, ECONOMIC AND REGIONAL. Cambridge: M.I.T. Press, 1969. xiiii, 1,040 p. Name Index, 993-996. Subject Index, 997-1040.

> This volume is an attempt by Isard to formulate a general theory for all of social science. He integrates the various disciplines into mathematical models and formulates a framework for a dy- namic general theory. The 16 chapters include discussions on such topics as "The Spatial Pattern of Decision-Making Authority and Organization," "Location Games With Applications to Classic Location Problems," "Some Background on General Social Systems," "General Equilibrium of the Economic Subsystem in a Multiregional Setting," and "On Alternative Approaches to Modeling Group Be- havior Within the General Theory."

Kain, John F. THE DISTRIBUTION AND MOVEMENT OF JOBS AND INDUS- TRY. Program on Regional and Urban Economics Discussion Paper, no. 8. Cambridge: M.I.T.-Harvard, Joint Center for Urban Studies, 1968. 73 p.

Lefeber, Louis. ALLOCATION IN SPACE: PRODUCTION AND TRANSPORT AND INDUSTRIAL LOCATION. Amsterdam: New Holland, 1968. xv, 151 p. Paper. Index.

> A general neoclassical approach is taken in this book, examining the spatial allocation of the factors of production and the allo- cation of goods. The study examines the framework for the choice of industrial location. A limited number of factors are included in the analysis.

Listokin, David. LAND USE CONTROLS: PRESENT PROBLEMS AND FUTURE REFORM. New Brunswick, N.J.: Transaction, 1974. 406 p. Index.

This is a series of essays examining current land use policies, the criticism of these policies, and the direction of policy changes which might be expected in the future.

Lösch, August. THE ECONOMICS OF LOCATION. Translated from the 2d rev. ed. by W.H. Woglom with the assistance of W.F. Stolper. New York: John Wiley and Sons, 1967. xxciii, 520 p. Subject Index, pp. 509-16. Name Index, pp. 517-20.

This original work in industrial location has provided the ground rules for location theorists of this generation. Lösch offers new insights into the work of von Thunen and critiques Weber's partial equilibrium analysis of location theory. He builds his own theory based on the work of Ohlin and Palander, thus setting the stage for the development of a dynamics of location.

Morgan, William E. TAXES AND THE LOCATION OF INDUSTRY. Boulder: University of Colorado Press, 1967. 30 p.

This is a study of the factors which influence industrial location. Both measurement and analysis of these factors is included in this study. Survey data from firms across the nation were analyzed with respect to the importance of labor, natural resources, and state and local taxes on location decisions.

Olsen, E. INTERNATIONAL TRADE THEORY AND REGIONAL INCOME DIFFERENCES: U.S. 1880-1950. Amsterdam: North Holland, 1971.

Pred, Alan. BEHAVIOR AND LOCATION: FOUNDATIONS FOR A GEO-GRAPHIC AND DYNAMIC LOCATION THEORY. Lund, Sweden: Royal University of Lund, Department of Geography, 1969. 152 p. No index.

A general model of location is formulated in these two volumes. Temporal changes within the behavorial aspects of the general model are discussed, as are the process of location in the agriculture, manufacturing, and tertiary sectors.

Webber, Michael J. IMPACT OF UNCERTAINTY ON LOCATION. Cambridge: M.I.T. Press, 1972. xviii, 310 p. References, pp. 283-300. Index, pp. 301-10.

This contribution to location theory goes "beyond being a critical analytical survey." Attention is focused on the impact of uncertainty in location decisions and on spatial patterns. A preliminary discussion on the way a new location theory may evolve is also put forth. Specific chapters deal with: "The Location Problem," "Analysis of Point Agglomeration," "Theories of Land Use," "Growth," "Decision Making Under Uncertainty," "A Least Risk Model of Town Formation," "Innovations, Learning and Location," and "Uncertainty, Location and Regional Economic Growth."

Wheat, L.F. REGIONAL GROWTH AND INDUSTRIAL LOCATION: AN
EMPIRICAL VIEWPOINT. Lexington, Mass.: Lexington Books, 1973. xii,
223 p. Notes, pp. 213-19. Index, pp. 219-23.

Six main hypotheses dealing with the factors which influence regional growth are examined by Wheat. Each is put forth, tested,
and correlates are presented. The work begins with a study of the
objectives, a presentation of regional growth patterns, and implications of recent studies. It then proceeds to a test of the main
hypotheses.

Wonnacott, Ronald J. MANUFACTURING COSTS AND THE COMPARATIVE
ADVANTAGE OF UNITED STATES REGIONS. Upper Midwest Study, Paper
no. 9. Minneapolis: University of Minnesota Press, 1963. viii, 83 p. Tables
and figures.

The purpose of this monograph is "to assemble information on inter-
area differences in industrial costs in the United States and analyze
the potential effects of these differences on the location of industry in the Upper Midwest." The analysis is of the average firm
with many, not all, production costs analyzed. There are major
discussions of wage rates, market potential, transportation costs,
and state and local taxes.

Chapter 14
REGIONAL MODELS AND TECHNIQUES

Bowers, John, and Woodward, V.H. THE ANATOMY OF REGIONAL ACTIVITY RATES AND REGIONAL SOCIAL ACCOUNTS FOR THE UNITED KINGDOM. Cambridge: Cambridge University Press, 1970. xiv, 171 p. Tables.

    Two papers published together examine measures and the measurement of regional economic activity in Britain.

Chen, David. A TABULAR SURVEY OF SELECTED REGIONAL ECONOMETRIC MODELS. Working Paper, no. 11. San Francisco: Federal Reserve Bank of San Francisco, 1972.

Conference on Research in Income and Wealth. INPUT-OUTPUT ANALYSIS: AN APPRAISAL. Princeton, N.J.: Princeton University Press, 1955. x, 377 p. Index, pp. 369-77.

    The object of these essays is to convey information and evaluate the tool-technique of input-output analysis. Written primarily for economists, I-O analysis is assessed as to its future uses and benefits. The problems of the approach are discussed along with the actual compilation of I-O tables.

Crow, R.T., et al. AN ECONOMETRIC MODEL OF THE BUFFALO SMSA. Buffalo: State University of New York at Buffalo, School of Management, 1973.

Czamanski, Stan. REGIONAL AND INTERREGIONAL SOCIAL ACCOUNTING. Lexington, Mass.: Lexington Books, 1973. xiv, 205 p. Notes, pp. 175-92. Bibliography, pp. 192-202. Index, pp. 203-5. Figures and tables.

    A comprehensive review of problems encountered in developing a regional accounting framework suggests that weaknesses arise from: (1) weaknesses in the tools in terms of quantifying the dollar value of public goods and services, (2) a lack of emphasis on stock phenomena, (3) the greater importance of disaggregated sectorial accounts for policy purposes, and (4) the lack of comprehensive systems. The second part of the book deals with the construction of regional input-output tables.

_____. REGIONAL SCIENCE TECHNIQUES IN PRACTICE. Lexington, Mass.: Lexington Books, 1972. 450 p. Bibliography. Index.

The tools and methods of regional science receive an in-depth treatment in this study of Nova Scotia. The attractiveness of this area lies in relative geographical isolation and political integration. Location factors, investment, and input-output analysis are thoroughly discussed, and a simple econometric model is put forth.

Czamanski, Stan, et al. AN ECONOMETRIC MODEL OF NOVA SCOTIA. Regional Studies Series, no. 2. Halifax, Canada: Institute of Public Affairs, Dalhousie University, 1968. ix, 236 p. Paper. No index.

This is a seven-sector econometric model of Nova Scotia which is based on several past studies. It includes a section discussing various types of regional models and the problems encountered in developing them.

Emerson, M. Jarvin. THE INTERINDUSTRY STRUCTURE OF THE KANSAS ECONOMY. Office of Economic Analysis and Kansas Department of Economic Development Planning Division Report, no. 21. Manhattan: Department of Economics, Kansas State University, 1969. vii, 221 p. No index.

This is an input-output study for the state of Kansas which develops the framework in historical, schematic, and mathematical terms. "State Economic Planning Models" and an "Impact Analysis" are generated from the study. Four wall-sized matrixes are appended.

Garnick, D.H., et al. TOWARD DEVELOPMENT OF A NATIONAL-REGIONAL IMPACT EVALUATION SYSTEM AND THE UPPER LICKING AREA PILOT STUDY. Regional Economics Division Staff Paper, no. 18. Washington, D.C.: U.S. Department of Commerce, 1971.

Ghosh, A., in collaboration with Chakrabarti, A. PROGRAMMING AND INTERREGIONAL INPUT-OUTPUT ANALYSIS: AN APPLICATION TO THE PROBLEM OF INDUSTRIAL LOCATION IN INDIA. Cambridge: Cambridge University Press, 1973. 104 p. References, p. 101. Index, pp. 102-04.

A programming model was used to specify capacity levels on the transportation system, existing and proposed new facilities and applied to the location of industry. An appendix deals with data sources and methods.

Giarratani, Frank; Maddy, James D.; and Socher, Charles E. REGIONAL AND INTERREGIONAL INPUT-OUTPUT ANALYSIS: AN ANNOTATED BIBLIOGRAPHY. Morgantown, W. Va.: University Library, 1976. 127 p. Author Index, pp. 123-27.

A variety of theoretical, conceptual, and applied sources dealing with input-output analysis are cited. Sources covering techniques, forecasting and simulation, impact analysis, environmental and water resource analysis, and urban studies are included as well.

Glickman, Norman J. ECONOMETRIC ANALYSIS OF REGIONAL SYSTEMS, EXPLORATIONS IN MODEL BUILDING AND POLICY ANALYSIS. New York: Academic Press, 1977. xi, 210 p. References, pp. 197-206. Index, pp. 207-10.

Glickman's study "assesses the role of econometric analysis in regional forecasting and policy analysis." A large-scale econometric model of the Philadelphia region forecasts output and employment by sector as well as wages, prices, and income. A set of government macro policy variables were also tested in the model. These included defense expenditures and revenue sharing. Major segments of the book, aside from the introduction, include, "Methods of Regional Economic Analysis," "A Forecasting Model," and "Testing the Model and Some Policy-Analytic Simulation Experiments."

Greenhut, Melvin L. A THEORY OF THE FIRM IN ECONOMIC SPACE. New York: Appleton-Century-Crofts, 1970. xiv, 389 p. Index, pp. 381-89.

While Greenhut accepts the insights of pure economic theory, he perceives them to be unrealistic and sets out to look at the uncertainty brought about by firms separated by space. He attempts to resolve this "theoretical chaos." The book consists of sixteen chapters which make up the four main parts of the book. Part I examines the "Impacts of Economic Space on Micro-Economic Theory." Part II deals with "Prices and Resource Allocation." Part III with "Spatial Distribution," and part IV covers "General Equilibrium, Welfare, and Social Policy."

Greenhut, Melvin L., and Ohta, H. THEORY OF SPATIAL PRICING AND MARKET AREAS. Durham, N.C.: Duke University Press, 1975. xi, 262 p. Mathematical Notes, pp. 241-58. Index, pp. 259-62.

The element of space is introduced into micro and macro theory in an analysis that "demonstrates the meaning of economic space and its impact on market types and price strategies and their interrelations with market area sizes and shapes under conditions of spatial monopoly and competition." Current economic theory is reviewed and synthesized. Eleven chapters are divided into four main parts: "Regional Economics, Facets of Space," "Nondiscriminatory and Discriminatory Pricing: The Monopoly Case," "Nondiscriminatory and Discriminatory Pricing: The Competitive Oligopoly Case," and "Spatial Configurations and Nondiscriminatory and Discriminatory Pricing."

Grimes, R. AN ECONOMETRIC MODEL OF GEORGIA. Athens: University of Georgia Press, 1973.

Hamilton, H.R.; Goldstein, S.E.; Milliman, J.W.; Pugh, A.L.; Roberts, E.B.; and Zellner, A. SYSTEMS SIMULATION FOR REGIONAL ANALYSIS: AN APPLICATION TO RIVER-BASIN PLANNING. Cambridge: Harvard University Press, 1969. xii, 407 p. Index, pp. 395-407.

> This work is the outgrowth of a series of reports dealing with the economic growth of the Susquehanna River Basin. The "methodology (of the study) is unique" and, therefore, perhaps of interest. In addition to reviewing mathematical models, the region, and the sectors used, a simulation of the model and implications for future research is generated.

Harmston, Floyd K., and Lund, Richard E. APPLICATIONS OF AN INPUT-OUTPUT FRAMEWORK TO A COMMUNITY ECONOMIC SYSTEM. University of Missouri Studies, vol. 42. Columbia: University of Missouri Press, 1967. xi, 124 p. Notes, pp. 108-9. Bibliography, pp. 110-16. Index, pp. 117-24.

> This fifteen sector input-output table is constructed for a hypothetical community of 20,000, and it is used as an illustration in a small community setting.

Isard, Walter, and Langford, Thomas W. REGIONAL INPUT-OUTPUT STUDY: RECOLLECTIONS, REFLECTIONS, AND DIVERSE NOTES ON THE PHILADELPHIA EXPERIENCE. Cambridge: M.I.T. Press, 1971. xvii, 228 p. Index, pp. 223-28. Bibliographical references at the end of chapters.

> The authors discuss their experiences in their project in Philadelphia that produced a 500-600 sector regional I-0 study. They look at their choices of the region, the base year, and the classification system along with survey procedures, dealing with secondary production and the construction of coefficients.

Laidlaw, C.D. LINEAR PROGRAMING FOR URBAN DEVELOPMENT. PLAN EVALUATION. New York: Praeger, 1972. xiv, 283 p. Selected References, pp. 279-83. No index.

> Five case studies are presented to illustrate how linear programming may be used to evaluate planning and urban development alternatives. The cases from Baltimore and Jersey City are urban renewal programming, intensive housing development evaluation, large-scale community development evaluation, airport system programming, and urban renewal design.

Lee, Tong Hun; Moore, John R.; and Lewis, David P. REGIONAL AND INTER-REGIONAL INTERSECTORAL FLOW ANALYSIS. THE METHOD AND APPLICATION TO THE TENNESSEE ECONOMY. Knoxville: University of Tennessee Press, 1972. vii, 164 p. Bibliography, pp. 159-61. Index, pp. 162-64.

> This report describes the construction of a three-region intersectoral model for the state of Tennessee. The model employs a rows only approach. The seven chapters are devoted to discussions of:

"Recent Developments in Interindustry Analysis," "Approach to Empirical Implementation," "The Statewide Model: The Empirical Results," "The Interregional Model: The Empirical Results," a "Summary," and "Conclusions."

Mera, Koichi. AN EQUILIBRIUM MODEL OF REGIONAL GROWTH: THE CASE OF THE UNITED STATES. Cambridge: Harvard University, Program on Regional and Urban Economics, 1970. 131 p. References, pp. 129-31.

This paper examines elements which make growth rates vary among regions and asks the question: "Is it possible to change the growth rate of a region by a policy decision at a regional level?" The approach assumes a perfect mobility of labor and capital and seeks to explain growth differentials.

_____. REGIONAL PRODUCTION FUNCTIONS AND REDISTRIBUTION POLICIES: THE CASE OF JAPAN. Cambridge: Harvard University, Program on Regional and Urban Economics, 1969. 124 p. References, pp. 123-4.

The regional distribution of income in Japan is examined as the economy and national income has grown.

_____. A STUDY OF THE NATION-WIDE REGIONAL ECONOMETRIC MODEL: COMMENTS AND SURVEY OF MODEL BUILDING FOR REGIONAL ECONOMICS. Discussion Paper, no. 55. Cambridge: Harvard University, Program on Regional and Urban Economics, 1969. 18 p.

This is a mathematical discussion of the role of predictive growth models.

Miernyk, William H. THE ELEMENTS OF INPUT-OUTPUT ANALYSIS. New York: Random House, 1967. xi, 156 p. Index, pp. 153-56.

Input-output analysis is explained in entirely nonmathematical terms. The last chapter uses elementary math in its description of an I-0 model. The book is designed to explain how input-output techniques work, not how to do an input-output study.

_____. SIMULATING REGIONAL ECONOMIC DEVELOPMENT: AN INTER-INDUSTRY ANALYSIS OF THE WEST VIRGINIA ECONOMY. Lexington, Mass.: Lexington Books, 1970. xxii, 337 p. Matrix Tables, pp. 239-326. Selected Bibliography, pp. 327-32. Notes, pp. 333-37. No index.

This work discusses the use of input-output models to simulate the process of regional economic development. The focus is on the method and demonstrates the flexibility of input-output models as useful tools. It permits the evaluation of the costs and benefits of a broad range of investment alternatives.

Miernyk, William H.; Bonner, Ernest; Chapman, John H., Jr.; and Shellhammer, Kenneth. IMPACT OF THE SPACE PROGRAM ON A LOCAL ECONOMY: AN INPUT-OUTPUT ANALYSIS. Morgantown: West Virginia University Press, 1967. 167 p. Appendixes, pp. 133-61. Index, pp. 163-67.

This book reports the NASA-Boulder, Colorado, project. The case is examined in historical perspective, and a preliminary export-base analysis is made. The framework for the sectors to be studied is set up, the data sources are elaborated, and the analysis is made. The results indicate the income and employment creating power of the space sector in a community.

Miernyk, William H., and Sears, John T. AIR POLLUTION ABATEMENT AND REGIONAL ECONOMIC DEVELOPMENT: AN INPUT-OUTPUT ANALYSIS. Lexington, Mass.: xvi, 194 p. Selected Annotated Bibliography, pp. 169-81. Index, pp. 189-94.

An "economics and engineering" approach is taken in this study with the focus on regional economic development not environmental management. A dynamic input-output model is used to examine the "effects clean air legislation would have on programs designed to stimulate the development of regions characterized by economic stagnation or slow economic growth." The volume is based on a two-year study in West Virginia.

Morrison, W.I., and Smith, P. INPUT-OUTPUT METHODS IN URBAN AND REGIONAL PLANNING: A PRACTICAL GUIDE. Progress in Planning Series, vol. 7. Elmsford, N.Y.: Pergamon Press, 1977. 122 p. Bibliography, pp. 99-105. Index, pp. 105-22.

While written for the urban planner, this monograph essentially elaborates the use of I-0 technique in the urban and regional economy. An understanding of the local economy is stressed, as is the use of this technique for economic analysis.

Nijkamp, Peter. PLANNING OF INDUSTRIAL COMPLEXES BY MEANS OF GEOMETRIC PROGRAMING. Rotterdam: Rotterdam University Press, 1972. x, 146 p. References, pp. 140-44. Index, pp. 145-46.

A number of development programs are set up that are "reasonable in a mixed economic setting, and are amenable to mathematical solutions." The four main topics of discussion are "Growth Poles and Industrial Complex Analysis," "Geometric Programing," "A Minimum Investment Model," and the "Alternative Objectives and Dynamics: A Dynamic Growth Model."

Paelinck, Jean H.P., and Nijkamp, Peter. OPERATIONAL THEORY AND METHOD IN REGIONAL ECONOMICS. New York: Saxon House, Lexington Books, 1975. xiii, 473 p. Index, pp. 469-73.

The three goals of this text are the presentation of theories of

regional economists, the rigorous development of these ideas--
(propositions submitted to empirical testing), and the mastery of
the tools of regional economics. Included is a historical review
of location theory and the work of Von Thunen, Weber, Palander,
Losch and others, methodological discussions of measurement, input-
output analysis, and linear programing. It is for advanced students.

Polenske, Karen R. MULTIREGIONAL INPUT-OUTPUT ANALYSIS. Vol. 4.
Lexington, Mass.: Lexington Books, 1974. xix, 521 p. Bibliography, pp.
511-19.

The papers presented in this volume were selected from those read
at the 6th International Conference on Input-Output Techniques,
held in Vienna in 1974. Both theoretical developments and applications are represented in this collection. The seven parts of the
book contain papers on: "National Economic Development Studies,"
"Applications in Developing Countries," "Regional and Interregional
Studies," "Industrial Applications," "Studies on Energy and the
Environment," "International Trade Studies," and "Optimization
Models and Production Functions."

Ratajczak, D. A QUARTERLY ECONOMETRIC MODEL FOR CALIFORNIA.
Los Angeles: UCLA, Graduate School of Management, 1972.

Richardson, Harry W. INPUT-OUTPUT AND REGIONAL ECONOMICS. New
York: Halsted Press, 1972. 294 p. Bibliography, pp. 261-83. Name Index,
pp. 284-86. Subject Index, pp. 287-94.

Richardson outlines the advantages and disadvantages of input-
output techniques for the regional scientist. The book examines the
scope and limitations of the input-output approach in relatively
nontechnical terms. The book is divided into three main parts:
"Theory," "Data Problems," and "Applications."

Richter, Charles. AN ECONOMETRIC MODEL OF THE COASTAL PLAINS
STATES. Chapel Hill: University of North Carolina, Department of Economics,
1971.

Rogers, Andrei. MATRIX ANALYSIS OF INTERREGIONAL POPULATION
GROWTH AND DISTRIBUTION. Berkeley and Los Angeles: University of
California Press, 1968. xiv, 110 p. Index, pp. 117-19.

This book illustrates how input-output analysis, statistical analyses,
and models of linear programing may be used to develop interregional and intraregional models of growth and development. Computations are emphasized rather than theorems and proofs. Characteristic roots and vectors are used in the analysis of stable states in
demographic and economic models. References and exercises are
found at the end of each chapter.

Rogers, Andrei. MATRIX METHODS IN URBAN AND REGIONAL ANALYSIS. San Francisco: Holden-Day, 1971. xiii, 508 p. Index, pp. 500–08.

This book illustrates how intraregional models of growth and development, input-output analysis, statistical analyses, and models of linear programing may be utilized in the teaching of urban and regional analysis. Computations are emphasized in the book with characteristic roots and vectors used to analyze stable states in economic models. References and exercises conclude each chapter.

Saigal, J.C. THE CHOICE OF SECTORS AND REGIONS. Rotterdam: Rotterdam University Press, 1966. 96 p. Symbols, pp. 93–94. Author Index, p. 95. Subject Index, p. 96.

The technique of planning sectors and regions for design of policy and planning are discussed. The sectors are appraised, criteria for the choice of sectors are put forth, as is the "Optimum path of development." A programing model is given, and transportation costs are introduced.

Schaffer, William A., et al. INTERINDUSTRY STUDY OF THE HAWAIIAN ECONOMY. Honolulu: Department of Planning and Economic Development, State of Hawaii, 1972. 104 p.

There are 54 industry sectors used in this interindustry model of the state of Hawaii. The study reviews input-output analysis, characterizes the Hawaiian economy, and presents the conclusions of the study.

Scientific American. THE INPUT/OUTPUT STRUCTURE OF THE AMERICAN ECONOMY. San Francisco: W.H. Freeman and Co., 1970.

An 8-color 70" x 46" wall chart with 5 off prints about I-0 analysis.

Scott, Alan J. COMBINATORIAL PROGRAMING SPATIAL ANALYSIS AND PLANNING. London: Methuen, 1971. vii, 204 p. Bibliography, pp. 166–95. Index, pp. 196–204.

This work surveys modern combinatorial programming methods and their application in urban and regional analysis. Special emphasis is placed on spatially structured problems. Topics discussed include: heuristic and exact methods of solving combinatorial programming problems, spatially structured combinatorial programs, transportation and transshipment problems, network analysis, location-allocation systems, and partitioning problems.

Stevens, B.T., and Trainer, G.A. THE GENERATION OF ERROR IN REGIONAL INPUT-OUTPUT MODELS. Philadelphia: Regional Science Research Institute, 1976.

Suits, D.B., et al. ECONOMETRIC MODEL OF MICHIGAN. Ann Arbor: University of Michigan, Department of Economics, 1966.

Takayama, T., and Judge, G.G. SPATIAL AND TEMPORAL PRICE EQUILIB-RIUM AND ALLOCATION MODELS. Amsterdam: North Holland, 1971. xx, 528 p. Author Index, pp. 522-24. Subject Index, pp. 525-28.

> This work is "concerned with the specification of a model that may be employed in analyzing pricing and allocation over space and time." The 20 chapters and 12 appendixes are broken into five parts which examine: "Mathematical Programing and Competi-tive Equilibrium," "Linear Programing and Allocation Models," "Single Product and Spatial Price Equilibrium Models," "Multiple Product and Spatial Price Equilibrium Models," and "General Competitive Spaceless and Spatial Equilibrium Models."

Tiebout, Charles M. THE COMMUNITY BASE STUDY. Supplementary Paper, no. 16. New York: Committee for Economic Development, 1962. 84 p. No index.

> The method of examining the local economy through the extension of economic base analysis to income and employment theory is set forth. Part I develops a "Guide to Base Studies," discussing such factors as the importance of understanding the community base, the use of a base study, and how one is begun. Part II deals with "Economic Base Analysis," itself examining the structure of the local economy and measuring it, the structural relations, and fore-casting community economic levels.

Tuck, B.H. AN AGGREGATE INCOME MODEL FOR A SEMI AUTONOMOUS ECONOMY. Fairbanks: Federal Field Committee for Development Planning in Alaska, 1967.

Van Duijn, Jacob J. AN INTERREGIONAL MODEL OF ECONOMIC FLUC-TUATIONS. Lexington, Mass.: Lexington Books, 1973. 200 p. Index.

> Cyclical movements are examined to deal with the questions of instability of output and employment in the context of regional economic characteristics and in examining governmental policies which might help regions cope with these fluctuations. An inter-regional model demonstrates the "regulatory influence of centrally directed economic activities over particular regions of the country." Chapter headings include: "The Interregional Model"; "National Averages of the Model Simulations"; "Trends in the Prototype Mod-el"; "Optional Distribution of Government Expenditure"; "Variation on the Trade Pattern"; "Migration"; and "The Timing of Changes in Government Expenditure in a Cyclical Economy."

Wilson, A.G. ENTROPY IN URBAN AND REGIONAL MODELING. London: Pion, 1970. 166 p. Appendixes, pp. 131-62. Author Index, pp. 163-64. Subject Index, pp. 165-66.

Multidisciplinary in perspective, this book's eight chapters deal with "Introduction," "What is Entropy," "Transportation Models," "Interregional Commodity Flows," dealing with gravity and input-output, "Location Models," "Problems of Missing or Additional Information in Flow and Location Models," "The Use of Entropy in the Analysis of Utility," and "Entropy, Social, Physical and General Systems Theory."

_____. URBAN AND REGIONAL MODELS IN GEOGRAPHY AND PLANNING. New York: John Wiley and Sons, 1974. xiv, 418 p. Bibliography. Index.

The aim of this work is "to give mainly an elementary account of the range of mathematical models used in the analysis and planning of cities and regions." A multidisciplinary, comprehensive approach is used in the development of a formal model and its test. The theory set forth is that of the structure and development process in cities and regions. Part III handles the "main core" of the analysis, and part II deals with the preliminaries. Part I provides a general introduction to urban and regional problems and methods, while part IV concludes by examining the use of models.

Chapter 15

COLLECTIONS OF ARTICLES, PAPERS, AND ESSAYS

Advanced Seminar in Economic Development. GROWTH CENTERS AND ECO-
NOMIC DEVELOPMENT, PROCEEDINGS. Austin, Tex.: Lyndon B. Johnson
School of Public Affairs, University of Texas, 1974. vii, 114 p.

> This book contains several papers relating to growth center strategy
> in the regional economic development process.

Bagwatti, J., and Eckaus, R.S., eds. DEVELOPMENT AND PLANNING:
ESSAYS IN HONOR OF PAUL ROSENSTEIN RODAN. London: Allen and
Unwin, 1973. 343 p. Index, pp. 314-36. Bibliography, pp. 336-43.

> Seventeen essays are presented on a variety of development-related
> topics. These include: "Growth of Development Economics" (2
> essays), "Development and Planning" (5 essays), "Income Distribu-
> tion and Regional Development" (3 essays), "Development and In-
> ternational Trade" (3 essays), "Cost-Benefit Analysis" (1 essay),
> "Labor Productivity" and "Value Theory."

Bendavid-Val, Avrom, and Waller, Peter P., eds. ACTION-ORIENTED AP-
PROACHES TO REGIONAL DEVELOPMENT PLANNING. New York: Praeger,
1975. xiii, 135 p. No index. Tables, charts, and maps.

> Papers whose focus range from the methodology to the techniques
> of the trade are presented. All are approaches or applications to
> regional development planning.

Blunden, John; Brook, Christopher; Edge, Geoffrey; and Hay, Alan, eds.
REGIONAL ANALYSIS AND DEVELOPMENT. New York: Harper and Row,
1973. 318 p. Index, pp. 314-18.

> This is a collection of 27 papers and readings covering a variety
> of topics of interest to geographers, planners, and economists.
> Both macro and micro approaches are included as are sections on
> measures of regional inequality and government intervention. This
> book grew out of the open university course of the same name and
> is designed for a 16-unit course.. Contributors include: E.L.
> Ullman, D.C. North, W.H. Miernyk, V. Fuchs, A. Pred, and
> R. Richardson.

Chatterji, M., ed. SPACE LOCATION + REGIONAL DEVELOPMENT. London: Pion, 1976. 239 p. No index.

There are sixteen original essays reporting on research into the spatial aspects of regional development in this book. Papers are by economists, geographers, and planners alike. Suggested uses are for graduate courses in specific disciplines or for senior undergraduates and practicing public planners.

Chisholm, Michael; Frey, Allan E.; and Haggett, Peter. REGIONAL FORECASTING. Proceedings of the 22d Symposium of the Colston Research Society held at the University of Bristol in 1970. London: Butterworths, 1971. x, 470 p.

Essays in the areas of economics, geography, and planning are found in this volume. The first group of essays deal with statistical methods used in forecasting. The second group are on the general area of forecasting for socioeconomic systems. Forecasting applications for the United Kingdom is the theme of essays in the third section.

Clout, Hugh, ed. REGIONAL DEVELOPMENT IN WESTERN EUROPE. New York: John Wiley and Sons, 1975. 328 p. Index, pp. 321-28.

Regional problems of Western Europe is the focus of this group of readings, as are the planning programs which have been developed to combat them. The first group of readings, all authored by Clout, examine the "Economic and Social Trends in Western Europe." There are four essays in this section which focus on development, population, energy, and rural areas. The second set of readings look at "Regional Development in Practice." The policies of ten Western European countries are explored in this section.

Committee for Economic Development. COMMUNITY ECONOMIC DEVELOPMENT EFFORTS: FIVE CASE STUDIES. Supplementary Paper, no. 18. New York: 1964. 349 p. No index.

There are six essays included in this volume which examines several communities which suffered prolonged unemployment during the 1950s. These studies discuss the recovery attempts in these areas which included inducing new industry to establish in the area, revitalizing and improving community facilities and retraining programs. Essays included are: "Community Adjustment" by J. Nixon, "The Economic Redevelopment of the Burlington, VT Area" by D. Gilmore, "Economic Development Efforts in the Utica-Rome, NY Area" by V.C. Crisafulli, "Chronic Unemployment in Altoona, PA" by J. Kaufman and H. Jones, "Economic Redevelopment for Evansville, IN" by J. Milliman and W. Pinnell, and "Helena-West Helena, AR" by W.P. Brann.

Cripps, E.L., ed. REGIONAL SCIENCE: NEW CONCEPTS AND OLD PROB-LEMS. London: Pion (distributed by Academic Press), 1975. 206 p. Illus.

> This is a collection of papers from the sixth annual conference of the British Section of the Regional Science Association held in London in 1972. The topic areas which these papers cover are: problems in the theory and practice of industrial location, further use of models in regional planning, new approaches to urban and regional modeling, and empirical enhancement of urban and regional models.

_____. SPACE-TIME CONCEPTS IN REGIONAL AND URBAN ECONOMICS. London: Pion, 1974. 237 p. No index.

> These papers are from the fifth annual conference of the British Section of the Regional Science Association. The first group of essays in these proceedings deal with space and time in regional science. The second deals with "Conventional Modes of Regional Economics." The third and fourth sections are devoted to papers on abstract models which rely on theory and analytical methods. The papers in section 5 deal with the spatial organization of cities and regions.

Dacey, Michael F., et al. ONE DIMENSIONAL CENTRAL PLACE THEORY. Northwestern University Studies in Geography, no. 21. Evanston, Ill.: Northwestern University Press, 1976.

> This book contains contributions by: M. Dacey, Flowerdew, Huff, Ko, and Pipkin.

Dean, Robert D.; Leahy, William H.; and McKee, David L., eds. SPATIAL ECONOMIC THEORY. New York: Free Press, 1970. ix, 365 p. Index, pp. 357-65.

> This is a collection of the "more important" articles in the area of spatial patterns of economic activity written since the 1940s. After general introductory essays by E. Hoover and L. Moses, the book devotes three essays to "Least Cost Theory," and three to "Locational Interdependence." Four essays examine "Market Area Analysis," and "Locational Equilibrium Analysis." "General Equilibrium Theory" contains three essays. Contributors include: W. Isard, H. Hotelling, F. Fetter, M. Greenhut, W. Alonso, E. Dunn, P. Samuelson, and S. Enke.

Federal Reserve Bank of Minneapolis. REGIONAL ECONOMIC POLICY: PRO-CEEDINGS OF A CONFERENCE. Minneapolis: 1974. 38 p. No index.

> This collection contains six papers on regional economic policy in various countries, the world, and economic region. Contributors include: G. Tolley and J.L. Gardner, B. Chinitz, K. Boulding, J. Rhodes, and B. Moore.

Firestone, O.J., ed. REGIONAL ECONOMIC DEVELOPMENT. Social Science Studies, no. 9. Ottawa: University of Ottawa Press, 1974. xi, 274 p. Bibliographical References and Index of Authors, pp. 273-74.

These are papers from a conference on regional economic development held in March, 1972. Included in the 14 selections are: "Critique of Regional Growth" by H. Richardson, "Urban Economics, New Approaches" by B. Chinitz, "Regional Development Policies" by J.P. Frances, and "Regional Economics and Social Disparity" by O.J. Firestone.

Friedmann, John, and Alonso, William, eds. REGIONAL DEVELOPMENT AND PLANNING: A READER. Cambridge: M.I.T. Press, 1964. xvii, 722 p. A Guide to the Literature, pp. 703-21.

This is one of the more useful collections of readings of early work in regional studies. The 35 reprinted articles are divided under four main parts. These are: "Space and Planning," "Location and Spatial Organization," "Theory of Regional Development," and "National Policy for Regional Development." Contributors are from a "who's who" of regional development literature with many "classic" articles. Authors include: F. Perroux, L. Rodwin, J. Friedmann, W. Alonso, A. Lösch, B.J.L. Berry, E. Ullman, H. Perloff, and L. Wingo, D. North, C. Tiebout, R. Baldwin, E. Lampard, C. Leven, E. Hoover, and B. Chinitz.

_____. REGIONAL POLICY: READINGS IN THEORY AND APPLICATIONS. Cambridge: M.I.T. Press, 1974. 835 p. Index.

This is the revised edition of REGIONAL DEVELOPMENT AND PLANNING: A READER by the same authors. The contents are quite different, with only seven of the thirty-seven readings common to both. The first four parts are devoted to readings on the concepts of space and development, the role of cities in national development, issues in regional development policy, and case studies in regional planning. The last part is a bibliographical essay on the last decade in regional development planning.

Gilbert, A.G., ed. DEVELOPMENT PLANNING AND SPATIAL STRUCTURE. New York: John Wiley and Sons, 1976.

Hansen, Niles M., ed. GROWTH CENTERS IN REGIONAL DEVELOPMENT. New York: Free Press, 1972. 298 p.

Eleven papers on growth centers are presented in this volume. They include: "Urban Growth Strategies Reconsidered" by L. Rodwin, "On Growth Poles" by J. Lasuen, "Growth Pole Theory: An Examination of Some of Its Basic Concepts" by M. Thomas, "A General Theory of Polarized Development" by J. Friedmann, "Hierarchial Diffusion: The Basis of Developmental Filtering and Spread in a

System of Growth Centers" by B. Berry, "Programming a Viable Minimal Investment Industrial Complex for a Growth Center" by J. Paelinck, "Development Poles and Related Theories: A Synoptic Review" by T. Hermansen, "Growth Pole Policy in Canada" by B. Higgins, "Spontaneous Growth Centers in Twentieth-Century American Urbanization" by W. Alonso and E. Medrich, "Growth Center Policy in the United States" by N. Hansen, and "Employment Growth and Changes in Unemployment at the County Level" by G. Laber.

———. PUBLIC POLICY AND REGIONAL ECONOMIC DEVELOPMENT: THE EXPERIENCES OF NINE WESTERN COUNTRIES. Cambridge, Mass.: Ballinger, 1974. xviii, 354 p. Bibliography, pp. 335-54. Tables, figures, maps. (No index.)

Theoretical and empirical essays are brought together in this collection which focuses on the attempts of governments to alter the spatial allocation of resources. Historical, social, and institutional perspectives are presented. Countries examined include the United States, West Germany, Italy, the Netherlands, Spain, and Canada. G. Cameron, T. Brevis, and N. Hansen are among the contributors.

Holland, Stuart, ed. BEYOND CAPITALIST PLANNING. New York: St. Martin's Press, 1978. vii, 222 p. Contributors, pp. 203-04. References, pp. 205-14. Index, pp. 215-22.

Contributors from four Western European countries examine planning in the context of a capitalist welfare state. The conclusion of these essays is that planning cannot work in this context, and that a new model of development, based on fundamental change in the mode and relations of productions, will be necessary. The ten essays are equally divided, examining "French Principles," "Italian Prospects," "German Perspectives," "British Malpractice," and "International Potential."

Isard, Walter, and Cumberland, John H., eds. REGIONAL DEVELOPMENT PLANNING: TECHNIQUES OF ANALYSIS. Paris: European Productivity Agency of OEEC, 1961. 450 p. Author Index, pp. 443-44. Subject Index, pp. 445-50.

Divided into three major parts, these readings explore: the regional, national, and institutional setting of development, the problems of regions in the process of economic development, and, finally, the analytical techniques used. Also included are introductions to the problem, a synopsis, and conclusion. Appendixes.

Judge, J.G., and Takayama, T., eds. STUDIES IN ECONOMIC PLANNING OVER SPACE AND TIME. Amsterdam: North Holland, 1973. xi, 727 p. Subject Index, pp. 724-27.

These 35 essays are divided into four major sections and several subsections. Part I examines "National and International Planning Models" in the context of "Economic Planning" (7 essays) and "Static and Dynamic Input-Output Models" (4 essays). Part II looks at "Linear Planning Models over Space and Time," and part III examines "Nonlinear Models over Space and Time." Essays in part IV discuss "Public and Private Planning Models." Contributors include: S. Czamanski, J. Tingergen, R. Frisch, and P. Samuelson.

Kain, John F., and Meyer, John R., eds. ESSAYS IN REGIONAL ECONOMICS. Cambridge: Harvard University Press, 1971. 412 p.

These eleven essays deal with the objectives of regional development policy, the impact of development, regional growth and capital flows, the special problems of the South, and regional models. It is "an application of the tools of economic analysis to policy problems." Contributors include: W. Alonzo, W. Miernyk, J. Kain, and G. Borts.

Karaska, Gerald J., and Bramhall, David F., eds. LOCATIONAL ANALYSIS FOR MANUFACTURING: A SELECTION OF READINGS. Cambridge: M.I.T. Press, 1969. xi, 515 p.

The intent of this group of readings is to fill the void that exists between abstract location theory and the very specialized studies dealing with a single location. Topic areas include: transportation costs, location costs, energy, and scale economies. Among the contributors are: W. Alonzo, B. Chinitz, O. Fuchs, W. Isard, and R. Vernon.

Karlqvist, A.; Lundqvist, L.; and Snickars, F., eds. DYNAMIC ALLOCATION OF URBAN SPACE. Lexington, Mass.: Saxon House, Lexington Books, 1975. xviii, 383 p. Figures and tables. No index.

This is a collection of papers generated by a conference of the same name held in Stockholm dealing with new methods to be used in the study of welfare and spatial structure. The approaches are general ones, to be used to examine agglomerations of many different kinds of activity occurring. Some 16 papers discuss topics ranging from fundamental issues in model building to spatial interaction models and the use of models in the planning process. There is also a section on welfare and competitive systems. It is mathematical in approach.

Kuklinski, A[ntoni]. R., ed. GROWTH POLES AND GROWTH CENTRES IN REGIONAL PLANNING. The Hague: Mouton, 1972. x, 306 p.

Some 15 essays examine "conceptual, theoretical and empirical case studies" in selected countries. Topics range from theory to regional planning practices.

Kuklinski, A[ntoni]. R., and Petrella, R., eds. GROWTH POLES AND RE-
GIONAL POLICIES: A SEMINAR. Paris: Mouton, 1972. viii, 267 p.

These papers were written for a conference on growth poles and
contain contributions dealing with the economic, social, geographic,
and institutional aspects. Contributions include: "Growth Poles in
Economic Theory and Policy" by L. Klaassen, "Growth Poles in
National Policy" by C. Frey, "The Concept of Polarized Development in Regional Planning" by T. DiTella, "Promemoria Concerning
Growth Center Policy Within the Framework of Swedish Policy" by
E. Bylund, and "Growth Poles in Underdeveloped Regions and Countries" by M. Penouil. A summary discussion and conclusions follow.

Ling, G.J.R., and Rimmer, P.J., eds. GOVERNMENT INFLUENCE AND
THE LOCATION OF ECONOMIC ACTIVITY. Canberra: The Australian National University, 1971. xv, 500 p.

This is a monograph of 21 essays dealing with "Government Spatial
Behavior," "Government Location and the Location of Agriculture
Industry," "Government Policy and Decentralization," and "The
Future Pattern of Cities."

Lo, Fu-Chen, and Salih, Kamal, eds. GROWTH POLE STRATEGY AND RE-
GIONAL DEVELOPMENT: ASIAN EXPERIENCES AND ALTERNATIVE AP-
PROACHES. New York: Pergamon Press for the United Nations Center for
Regional Development, 1978. xvi, 274 p. Index, pp. 271-74.

This volume brings together papers from a seminar focusing on a
"critical review of strategies and growth pole approaches to regional planning in Asia." Part I is devoted to case studies in
decentralization and growth pole approaches in Asia. Part II
examines "Alternative Approaches to Regional Development in Asia."
There are 11 essays in the volume.

McKee, David L.; Dean, Robert D.; and Leahy, William H., eds. REGIONAL
ECONOMICS: THEORY AND PRACTICE. New York: Free Press, 1970. viii,
264 p. Index, pp. 261-64.

This is a collection of readings which deal with major problems
at the regional level. There are five major parts to the volume
and 16 essays. Two essays introduce the subject and are followed
by four essays devoted to "Economic Theory and Regional Expansions."
Contributors to this section are D. North, J.C. Stabler, and M.
Greenhut. Part III deals with "Development Pole Theory" and contains essays by F. Perroux, A.O. Hirshman, and N.M. Hansen.
"Toward a Regional Equilibrium Analysis" is the topic of Part IV
with essays from W. Isard and G. Borts. B. Chinitz, N. Hansen,
and S. Robock suggest alternative "Regional Economic Policy" in
Part V.

Articles, Papers, and Essays

Needleman, L., ed. REGIONAL ANALYSIS: SELECTED READINGS. Baltimore: Penguin Books, 1968. 398 p. Further Reading, pp. 383-86. Acknowl-
edgements, pp. 387-88. Author Index, pp. 389-92. Subject Index, pp. 393-
98.

> This is a collection of 11 articles and papers that "present some
> of the concepts and tools of regional analysis, describe regional
> data and outline, and occasionally test, regional economic models
> of trade and development." The contributions include: "Regional
> Economics: A Survey" by J. Meyer, "Regional and Interregional
> Accounts in Perspective" by C. Leven, "Regional and Interregional
> Input-Output Models: An Appraisal" by C. Tiebout, "Regional
> Inequality and the Process of National Development" by J. William-
> son, "Regional Growth and Maturity in the U.S." by G. Borts and
> J. Stein, "Development Policies for Southern Italy" by H. Chenery,
> "State and Regional Payments Mechanisms" by J. Ingram, "A Re-
> gional Test of the Heckscher-Ohlin Hypothesis" by J. Moroney and
> J. Walker, "Regional Aspects of Stabilization Policy" by S. Enger-
> man, "Location Theory" by W. Alonso, and "Further Calculations
> on Regional Differences in Profitability and Growth" by G. Fisher.

Papagiorgiou, George J., ed. MATHEMATICAL LAND USE THEORY. Lexington, Mass.: Lexington Books, 1976. xx, 311 p. A Coded Bibliography of
the New Urban Economics, pp. 293-307. Figures and tables.

> This is one of the earliest collections of work in the "new urban
> economics." The first part contains three general statements on
> mathematical land use theory, and the second part contains 15
> essays on specific problems in the field.

Perlman, Mark; Leven, Charles L.; and Chinitz, Benjamin, eds. SPATIAL,
REGIONAL AND POPULATION ECONOMICS: ESSAYS IN HONOR OF EDGAR
M. HOOVER. New York: Gordon and Breach, 1972. ix, 399 p. Biblio-
graphical references at the end of each essay.

> There are sixteen essays on a variety of urban-regional issues, in-
> cluding input-output models, metropolitan and regional policy, the
> economy of the central city included. Contributors include: H.S.
> Perloff, M. Whitman, L. Wingo and J. Fisher, W. Isard and T.
> Smith, and B. Chinitz.

Real Estate Research Program. ESSAYS IN URBAN LAND ECONOMICS. Los
Angeles: UCLA, 1966.

Richardson, Harry W. REGIONAL ECONOMICS: A READER. New York:
Macmillan Co., 1970. x, 245 p. Suggestions for Further Reading, pp. 231-
33. Notes on Contributors, pp. 234-38. Index of Names, pp. 239-42. Index
of Subjects, pp. 243-45.

> This book contains 16 articles on various topics in regional eco-
> nomics and policy from a wide spread of journals covering location,

regional macroeconomics, and policy issues. They include: "Losch on Location" by Stefan Valavanis, "Game Theory, Location Theory and Industrial Agglomeration" by Walter Isard, "Estimation of Differential Employment Multipliers in a Small Regional Economy" by S. Weiss and E. Gooding, "Regional Multipliers" by A.J. Brown, "The Construction of Interregional Business Cycle Models" by J. Airov, "Toward a Theory of Interregional Fiscal Policy" by A. Peacock, "Towards the Application of Dynamic Growth Theory to Regions" by L. Hartman and D. Seckler, "Regional Income Differences Within a Common Market" by E. Olsen, "Development Pole Theory in a Regional Context" by N. Hansen, "Long Range Forecasting with a Regional Input-Output Model" by W. Miernyk, "Appropriate Goals for Regional Economic Policy" by B. Chinitz, and "A Short Course in Model Design" by I. Lowry.

Robinson, E.A.G., ed. BACKWARD AREAS IN ADVANCED COUNTRIES. London: Macmillan Co., 1969. xviii, 474 p. Index, pp. 469-74.

These proceedings of a conference held by the International Economics Association consist of 19 papers. The conference, sponsored by the E.D.A., was held in Gaithersburg, Md., in April of 1972 and included presentations by B.J.L. Berry, I. Fisher, G. Torley, T.P. Skully, S.P. Dresch, and W. Alonso. These papers are included in the proceedings. Topics include "Regional Growth Center," "Behavorial Models of Inter-Regional Migration," "National Growth Policy and Environmental Effects of Cities," and "Policy Implications of Intermetropolitan Migration Flows."

Rodefield, Richard; Flora, Jan; Voth, Donald; Fujimoto, Isao; and Converse, Jim. CHANGES IN RURAL AMERICA: CAUSES, CONSEQUENCES AND ALTERNATIVES. St. Louis: C.V. Mosby Co., 1978. xvii, 550 p. Index, pp. 543-50.

Twelve chapters and over 100 readings make up this readings text. The major objective of the authors is "to provide the reader with a better understanding of changes in the rural sector."

Sant, M.C., ed. REGIONAL POLICY AND PLANNING FOR EUROPE. Farnborough, Engl.: Saxon House, 1974. xix, 268 p. No index.

This collection of papers examines regional economic policies and problems in Europe. They incorporate a number of ideas and topics, including: "Regional Economic Policy in the United Kingdom," "The Effects of Regional Economic Policy in the United Kingdom," "Regional Policy in the EEC," "European Regional Policies," "The National System of Cities as a Framework for Urban and Regional Policy," "European Integration, Urban Regions and Medium-Sized Towns," "Regional Policy and Sub-Regional Planning in the North West," "Regional Policies and Regional Government," "Center and

Region in Policy," "Objectives for Regional Policy: The View From Industry," and "Regional Policy and Planning: Future Research Priorities."

Senior, Derick, ed. THE REGIONAL CITY: AN ANGLO AMERICAN DIS-CUSSION OF METROPOLITAN PLANNING. Chicago: Aldine Publishing Co., 1966. xiii, 192 p.

These essays give an account of the United Kingdom's approaches to regional planning. The context for the essays range from structure and strategy to new towns, growth centers, and land use. Flexibility is one theme which persists throughout the collection, suggesting that growth strategies and programs must shift with technology.

Simons, R. Miles, ed. METROPOLITAN PROBLEMS, INTERNATIONAL ASPECTS: A SEARCH FOR COMPREHENSIVE SOLUTIONS. Toronto: Methuen, 1970. xx, 534 p.

These papers were commissioned by the Canadian government for a training program on metropolitan problems. Many aspects of the urban scene are covered from government, finance, and public services, to the demographic and economic aspects of the city.

Smith, Robert H.T.; Taffee, Edward J.; and King, Leslie J., eds. READINGS IN ECONOMIC GEOGRAPHY: THE LOCATION OF ECONOMIC ACTIVITY. Chicago: Rand McNally and Co., 1968. 406 p. Index, pp. 401-06.

The approach of this volume toward the location of economics is that of the economist and the geographer. Theoretical and empirical essays utilize both inductive and deductive methods. Part I on "Classical Location Theory" contains articles by M. Chisholm, E. Hoover, R.M. Haig, B.J.L. Berry, and A. Pred and S. Valavans. Part II contains 9 empirical studies in location, while Part III devotes 7 essays to a "Restatement of Theory." Six essays on "New Approaches in Empirical Analysis" round out the volume.

Sussman, Carl, ed. PLANNING THE FOURTH MIGRATION: THE NEGLECTED VISION OF THE REGIONAL PLANNING ASSOCIATION OF AMERICA. Cambridge: M.I.T. Press, 1976. xii, 277 p. Index, pp. 269-77.

This is an anthology devoted to resurrecting the "new approach to regional planning" of L. Mumford and others, which has not been met. Major sections deal with "Metropolitan Civilization: Its Rise and Fall," "The First Statewide Planning," "Regionalism: Some Ends and Means," and "Metropolitan versus Regional Planning."

Chapter 16
BIBLIOGRAPHIES OF REGIONAL ECONOMICS
AND INDUSTRIAL LOCATION

Baxtresser, Betty B.   NON-URBAN PATTERNS OF LAND UTILIZATION 1968-
1968. Washington, D.C.: National Agricultural Library, USDA, 1968.   iv,
39 p. Author Index, pp. 30-34. Subject Index, pp. 35-39.

> This is a bibliography which presents "selected references on cur-
> rent and projected patterns of non-urban land utilization and the
> effects of these patterns on rural growth, transportation, land val-
> ues, and regional planning."

Berry, Brian J.L., and Pred, Allen.   CENTRAL PLACE STUDIES: A BIBLIOG-
RAPHY OF THEORY AND APPLICATIONS.   Bibliography Series, no. 1.   Philadelphia: Regional Science Institute, 1965.   vi, 153 p. Index, pp. 139-47.

> This is a comprehensive coverage of the theory and empirical work
> relating to size, spacing, and the function of cities, trading areas,
> and others.

Bracket, C.A., and Stevens, B.H.   INDUSTRIAL LOCATION: A REVIEW
AND ANNOTATED BIBLIOGRAPHY OF THEORETICAL, EMPIRICAL AND CASE
STUDIES. Bibliography Series, no. 3. Philadelphia: Regional Science Research
Institute, 1967.   199 p.

> Some 854 entries are included in the comprehensive listing.

California. University of. Los Angeles. Real Estate Research Program.   IN-
DUSTRIAL LOCATION BIBLIOGRAPHY. Los Angeles: 1959.   ii, 82 p.   No
index.

> A wide array of topics are included in this listing, including:
> "Area Planning and Industrial Location," "Bibliographies," "Fac-
> tors in Industrial Location," "Financial Aspects of Location," "For-
> eign Industrial Location," "General," "Geography, Economic and
> Other," "Industrial Decentralization and Dispersion," "Industrial
> Growth and Expansion," "Industrial Location and the Community &
> Community Promotion," "Industrial Location and Resources," "In-

dustrial Location Surveys," "Industrial Location, U.S., Regional,
State, and City," "Location Theory," "National Security and Defense," "Planned Industrial Communities and Districts," "Relocation
of Industry," "Site Selection and Development," "Small Business,"
"Small Communities, Suburbanization and Non-Urban Areas," "Specific Industries and Industrial Location," "Taxation and Subsidization
of Industry," "Transportation and Industrial Location," "Urban Redevelopment and Industrial Location," "Zoning," and "Miscellaneous."

Hamilton, F.E. Ian. REGIONAL ECONOMIC ANALYSIS IN BRITAIN AND
THE COMMONWEALTH. London: Weidenfeld and Nicolson, 1969. viii,
410 p. Index to Journals, pp. 395-410.

The historical trends in regional planning and regionalism are discussed in the introduction to this nonannotated listing of some 5,117
sources.

International Institute for Environment and Development. HUMAN SETTLEMENTS:
AN ANNOTATED BIBLIOGRAPHY. Elmsford, N.Y.: Pergamon Press, 1976.
vii, 220 p. Subject Index, pp. 201-13. Author Index, pp. 213-16.

This volume was prepared for "Habitat," a U.N. conference on
human settlements held in Vancouver in 1976. The 1,720 entries
deal with work examining the problems encountered within urban
development. Human habitat is viewed as encompassing all aspects of the environment.

Meyer, John R. REGIONAL ECONOMICS: A SURVEY. Discussion Paper,
no. 17. Cambridge: Harvard University, 1967. 54 p. References, pp. 48-
54.

This is a review and summary of the literature in regional economics,
first published in the AMERICAN ECONOMIC REVIEW in March,
1963.

Pillai, N.G., et al. REGIONAL DEVELOPMENT AND ECONOMIC GROWTH,
PROBLEMS, ANALYSIS AND POLICIES: SELECTED BIBLIOGRAPHY. Ottawa:
Planning Division, Department of Regional Economic Expansion, 1969. 285 p.
Paper. No index.

Some 3,500 books, pamphlets, and journal articles are listed in
this volume. The nine chapters are devoted to "General Development," "Canada," "France," "Great Britain," "Italy," "Sweden,"
"United States," "Regional Development," and "Regional Development and Economic Growth."

Regional Economic Development Institute. A BIBLIOGRAPHY OF RESOURCE
MATERIALS IN THE FIELD OF REGIONAL ECONOMIC DEVELOPMENT. Washington, D.C.: U.S. Department of Commerce, 1966. 99 p.

All materials listed have a regional approach and are of use to regional economists. Articles, theses, and speeches are included, as is "A Suggested Classification Scheme for a Regional Economics Library." Census reports are excluded.

Richardson, Harry W. "The State of Regional Economics: A Survey Article." INTERNATIONAL REGIONAL SCIENCE REVIEW 3 (Fall 1978): 1-48.

Richardson updates Meyer's earlier review and comments on the strengths and weaknesses of various theories and approaches used in regional economics.

Townroe, P.M. INDUSTRIAL LOCATION AND REGIONAL ECONOMIC POLICY: A SELECTED BIBLIOGRAPHY. Birmingham, Engl.: Center for Urban and Regional Studies, University of Birmingham, 1968. vii, 43 p. Author Index, pp. 41-43.

Included in this bibliography are the most widely used books, articles, and papers in the field since 1960. No government material is included. While most of the sources are British, there are North American sources. Topics included are: location of industrial plants, regional analysis, regional problems, and regional policy measures.

Wheeler, James O. INDUSTRIAL LOCATION: A BIBLIOGRAPHY 1966-1972. Monticello, Ill.: Council of Planning Librarians Exchange Bibliography, 1973. 68 p.

This volume contains selected journals, articles, books and monographs, reports, bulletins, and Ph.D. dissertations in the field of industrial location.

Appendix
JOURNALS AND SERIES OF INTEREST
IN URBAN AND REGIONAL ECONOMICS

ANNALS OF REGIONAL SCIENCE. Bellingham, Wash.: Western Washington State College, College of Business and Economics, 1967-- . 3 per year.

CANADIAN JOURNAL OF REGIONAL SCIENCE. Halifax, Nova Scotia: Institute of Public Affairs, Dalhousie University, 1978-- . 2-4 per year.

ECONOMIC GEOGRAPHY. Worcester, Mass.: Clark University. 4 per year.

ENVIRONMENT AND PLANNING, SERIES A: URBAN AND REGIONAL RESEARCH. London: 8 Pion Ltd., 1969-- . 8 per year.

GROWTH AND CHANGE. Lexington, Ky.: College of Business and Economics, University of Kentucky, 1970-- . 4 per year.

INDIAN JOURNAL OF REGIONAL SCIENCE. Kharagpur, India: C.R. Pathak, Department of Architecture and Planning, Indian Institute of Technology, 1968-- . 2 per year.

INTERNATIONAL REGIONAL SCIENCE REVIEW. Philadelphia, Pa.: Regional Science Association, 1975-- . 2 per year.

JOURNAL OF REGIONAL SCIENCE. Philadelphia, Pa.: Regional Science Research Institute, 1958-- . 3 per year.

KARLSRUHE PAPERS IN REGIONAL SCIENCE. New York: Academic Press, 111 Fifth Avenue, New York, N.Y.

LAND ECONOMICS. Madison: University of Wisconsin.

LONDON PAPERS IN REGIONAL SCIENCE. London: Pion Ltd.; available from Academic Press, 111 Fifth Avenue, New York, N.Y.

NORTHEAST REGIONAL SCIENCE REVIEW. Binghampton, N.Y.: School of Management, SUNY, 1971-- . Annual.

PAPERS OF THE REGIONAL SCIENCE ASSOCIATION. Philadelphia: Regional Science Association, University of Pennsylvania, 1967-- . 2 per year.

REGIONAL SCIENCE AND URBAN ECONOMICS (formerly REGIONAL AND URBAN ECONOMICS). Amsterdam, The Netherlands: North-Holland Publishing Co., 1971-- . 3 per year.

REGIONAL SCIENCE PERSPECTIVES. Manhattan, Kans.: Department of Economics, Kansas State University, 1971-- . Annual.

REVIEW OF REGIONAL STUDIES. Clemson, S.C.: Clemson University, 1970-- . 3 per year.

Other journals which often publish titles in regional and urban economics are:

THE AMERICAN CITY

AMERICAN ECONOMIC REVIEW

BELL JOURNAL OF ECONOMICS

CANADIAN JOURNAL OF ECONOMICS

ECONOMETRICA

ECONOMIC DEVELOPMENT AND CULTURAL CHANGE

ECONOMIC JOURNAL

JOURNAL OF ECONOMIC LITERATURE

JOURNAL OF URBAN ECONOMICS

JOURNAL OF URBAN HISTORY

OXFORD ECONOMIC PAPERS

REVIEW OF ECONOMICS AND STATISTICS

SOUTHERN ECONOMIC JOURNAL

URBAN AFFAIRS QUARTERLY
URBAN RESEARCH NEWS
WESTERN ECONOMIC JOURNAL

There are several publishers with series in urban and regional economics. These include:

Arno Press
A New York Times Company
Three Park Avenue
New York, N.Y. 10016

Ballinger Publishing Co.
Cambridge, Mass. 02138

Center for Environmental Studies
62 Chandor Place
London WC2 N4H
England

Joint Center for Urban Studies of
   the Massachusetts Institute of
   Technology and Harvard University
53 Church Street
Cambridge, Mass. 02138

Lexington Books
125 Spring Street
Lexington, Mass. 12073

Pion Ltd.
order from:
Academic Press
111 Fifth Avenue
New York, N.Y. 10003

Praeger Publishers
111 Fourth Avenue
New York, N.Y. 10003

Sage Publications
P.O. Box 5024
Beverly Hills, Calif. 90210

INDEXES

AUTHOR INDEX

This index includes names of all editors, compilers, translators, and other contributors to works cited in the text. It is alphabetized letter by letter and numbers refer to page numbers.

Author Index

Author Index

Author Index

TITLE INDEX

This index includes titles of all books, monographs, published papers, and reports cited in the text. It is alphabetized letter by letter and numbers refer to page numbers.

Title Index

Title Index

Title Index

Title Index

Title Index

Title Index

Title Index

SUBJECT INDEX

This index is alphabetized letter by letter and numbers refer to page numbers.

Subject Index

Subject Index

Location and spatial organization
103, 127, 128, 144
Location theory 31, 61, 65, 87,
88, 93, 110, 123, 124, 126,
143, 146, 148, 150
and systems analysis 25
London 13
Lösch, August 119, 123, 149
Louisiana, economic development of
120

M

Markets
and economic space 133
and industrial location 125
and location theory 127
and urban land use 28
Marxist
approaches to urban problems 84
approaches to urban theory 20,
84
rent analysis 20
Massachusetts. See Boston; New
Bedford
Megalopolis 32
Mesoeconomic sectors 103
Methodology
in regional development 113, 118
and urban systems 77
Metropolitan area, international list
98
Metropolitan economy 21
Metropolitan functions 21
Metropolitan growth 20, 40, 42
Metropolitan policy 148
Metropolitan problems 3, 8, 13,
150
Michigan. See Detroit
Microeconomic, approaches to urban
affairs 90
Middle East 47
Military, effects of expenditures on
urban areas 112
Milwaukee, longitudinal study 27
Minneapolis 61
Minnesota. See Minneapolis
Missouri, personal income of
counties 121
See also St. Louis

Models
of land development 26
regional growth 105, 107, 134
regional planning 143
and spatial patterns 126
urban environment 25, 50, 82,
85
urban land use 24
of urban structure 83
Modern city 24
Moscow 13
Multivariate statistics 25
Municipal government functions 4

N

National Bureau of Economic
Research simulation model 39
National urban policy 81
Neighborhoods 48
Networks, urban 7
Newark 32
New Bedford, Mass. 47
New communities 24, 55
New Jersey, urban growth 35
See also Princeton
New towns 47, 51, 52
New Urban Economics 29, 148
New York. See Utica-Rome
New York City
city region 13, 22
location trends 38
metropolitan study 24
New York State
community development strategies
32
council of governments 120
functional region 121
See also Buffalo; Harlem
No-growth 21, 30
Nonmarket transfers in urban
society 65
Northeastern seaboard 22
Nova Scotia
I-O model 132

O

Oakland 40
Ohio. See Cleveland
Ontario, industrial structure 125

Subject Index

Subject Index